YOGA PSYCHOLOGY

YOGA PSYCHOLOGY
A Practical Guide to Meditation

Swami Ajaya, Ph.D.

The Himalayan Institute Press
Honesdale, Pennsylvania

The Himalayan Institute Press
RR 1 Box 405
Honesdale, PA 18431

© 1976 by The Himalayan International Institute of Yoga Science
and Philosophy of the U.S.A.

14   13   12   11   10   9   8

This book is printed on acid-free paper. ∞

Library of Congress Catalog Card Number: 76-374539

ISBN 0-89389-052-9

From our childhood onward we are taught to examine and verify the objects of the world. This system of education makes the mind flow outward. But yoga psychology makes us aware of ourselves on all levels and finally helps us in becoming established in our essential nature, which is peace, happiness, and bliss. Meditation is a systematic inward method which helps us in knowing all levels and ultimately the center of consciousness itself.

Sri Swami Rama of the Himalayas

Introduction

In the West we tend to view yoga in one of two ways— as a form of spiritual philosophy or as a technique of physical development. Only in recent years have we come to realize that yoga is also a psychological system and method for the expansion of consciousness enabling an individual to reach new levels of understanding and self-actualization. *Yoga Psychology* is thus a very refreshing and appropriate title for this book by Swami Ajaya.

Since the essential method of yoga psychology is meditation, Swami Ajaya discusses the process of meditation in considerable detail. Those who wish to practice meditation will find in this book a wealth of information not easily available in a single volume elsewhere. The book includes excellent in-depth discussions of the psychological effects of mantra upon human consciousness and the subjective changes that occur with continued practice of meditation. The author also includes a discussion of other substantive ideas, intrinsic not so much to the actual techniques of meditation, but which have a strong bearing on the process of expanding consciousness and reaching the highest levels of consciousness through meditation. These ideas, which are often a source of controversy in the West, such as the need to renounce worldly desires or to change one's well-ingrained dietary habits, are discussed in the context of individual psychological needs. Both the beginning and the advanced student of meditation will find that many of their questions have been anticipated and discussed by Swami Ajaya.

Som N. Ghei, Ph.D.
Professor of Psychology
University of Wisconsin,
Oshkosh

Contents

I

The Need for Meditation

What is Meditation?

There are many misconceptions regarding meditation and what one can achieve through meditation. New students of meditation are likely to have distorted expectations of the meditational experience. For example, those who have turned to meditation from drug experimentation may expect to see vivid colors and fantasies, to heighten their sense color experiences, or to feel something analogous to being "high." Since drug-taking and meditation are each described as consciousness-expanding, they may have the erroneous belief that consciousness is expanded in a similar manner by both.

Others who are more oriented toward problem solving think of meditation as contemplation. That is, they consider meditation to consist of sitting quietly and focusing the mind on some particular problem or concern in order to resolve the problem or gain deeper insight into it. If you are concerned about making a decision, you may say, "I'll meditate on it," meaning you will sit quietly for some time and think through all the aspects of the decision to be made. Or you may take a religious idea such as the concept "God is love" and "meditate" upon it by thinking about it from every possible angle so that the meaning of the phrase is understood and experienced. While in the West the two terms *meditation* and *contemplation* are often used interchangeably, in the East the practice of meditation is distinctly different from contemplation.

Others, whose thinking is more careless and scattered, may believe that meditation is simply a process of letting the mind drift from one thought to another without any specific direction. It is supposed that this aimless drifting will lead the mind to freedom from cares and worries.

When you have practiced meditation for some time, you will come to see that it is an experience very different from any described thus far. The purpose of meditation is not to get "high" or to have unusual experiences. Some students report seeing "funny colors moving around," or bright lights, or "a vision of a person" who spoke to them during meditation. A competent teacher will usually discourage students from becoming too interested in these distracting fantasies since they lead to mental confusion and turmoil instead of a calm, centered mind. Meditation goes beyond these sensory experiences and fantasies.

Meditation upon a problem is far more subtle and refined than contemplation, than merely thinking through a concern or idea. It is bringing your mind to a centered state and resting on a particular object given to you. It could be a sound, a word or any other object recommended by a spiritual teacher who is experienced in the path of meditation. Meditation and contemplation are two entirely different methods. The object of meditation cannot and should not be changed, but contemplation always centers upon different ideas, though in the same trend. The word *dhyanam* as used in yoga psychology and translated into English as meditation should not be taken as contemplation. *Dhyanam* or meditation is the final rung on the ladder of yoga to attain illumination or *samadhi.*

In meditation there is a definite goal, namely, to experience the highest state of consciousness and to feel greater joy and peace. Allowing the mind to simply drift where it will is contrary to these goals and the process of reaching them. If you let a boat drift in the water, it will be moved haphazardly by the winds and tides. Many people live their lives in this uncertain way. They pursue one thing for a while and then stop and decide, "This won't give me peace and happiness. I think I'll go in that direction instead." The practice of meditation takes you beyond this haphazard movement, along a path which enriches life and gives it more purpose and direction. It makes the mind one-pointed and inwardly directed. When a dissipated mind becomes one-pointed and inwardly directed, it has the capacity to penetrate into the deeper levels of the inner world.

Actually, meditation is neither like a drug experience nor like the contemplative resolution of particular concerns, nor the wandering of a non-directed mind. In order to understand what it is, we have to begin with an open mind which is ready to deal with new concepts and a new frame of reference. One should understand the whole technique, psychology and philosophy of meditation. One should learn to prepare himself and attain freedom from his previous notions, doubts, curiosities and fantasies before he steps onto this path.

Meditation is a method of training a disorderly,

disorganized mind to become proficient and creative. In one of the basic texts of yoga and meditation, Patanjali, the codifier of yoga science, defines meditation as the "controlling of the thought waves of the mind." The accomplishment of this task is the aim of the entire science of yoga. The science of meditation is as ancient as human existence, though it was developed in a scientific manner some 5,000 years ago in India. At that time, very wise people began to explore their true nature by asking such fundamental questions of life as "Who am I?" "What is the purpose of life?" and "Why do I exist?"

In order to find the right answers, the sages of ancient times experimented with various approaches to self-study and discovered certain definite methods of meditation. The *Svetasvatara Upanishad* says, "Those great sages . . . with the help of meditational techniques found out the mystery of life and the universe."

By using the tool of introspection, they tried to put the whole complex puzzle into a meaningful order. They watched the way their feelings and thoughts arose, the way they became interested in certain things, what made them miserable and unhappy, and what made them feel joyous. They delved deeper and deeper into the subtle workings of the mind and found that the more they explored, the calmer their minds become. They began to find that through this process they could reach new levels of consciousness.

As they continued in their self-study, their sensitivity to experiences of body and mind greatly increased. As they learned to sit quietly for long periods of time, they began to observe how thoughts arose in their minds, then led to emotions and finally to actions. Through such study of the internal states, these ancient sages began to become aware of the way in which the workings of the mind and the body were controlled. They were then able to alter their mental and physical states at will.

After the great masters had gone through this process of self-study, they taught what they had learned to those students who came to them. In the days before books, the science of meditation was passed from master to student in the oral tradition. The students would verify what was taught through their own experience, and would then extend the knowledge even further through their own experiments in consciousness. This process which was used for developing a body of knowledge about the mind is similar to the way the modern scientists work, extending the fund of knowledge through experimentation and passing on their findings to students and colleagues who test their results and experiment further. Meditation is an exact science. The science of meditation is an experimental study of inner processes comparable to our modern sciences, whose field of study is primarily external events.

The Essential Unity of Various Forms of Meditation

To the beginning student there may seem to be many different forms of meditation. He hears about Zen meditation, superconscious meditation, transcendental meditation and many other varieties. He learns that while the Zen Buddhist monk sits quietly with his eyes partially opened, looking at a blank wall, the yoga meditator sits with eyes closed, concentrating on a particular word, thought, or image. These superficial differences in behavior may lead the beginning student to confusion and uncertainty about whether meditation is one practice or many. Actually, at the deepest level, all meditation involves the same process of centering the mind on a particular thought or object, and all meditational forms come from the same historical source.

The Sanskrit word for meditation is *dhyanam*. Starting in India and tracing the development of this term and its use in various cultures, we can see how the spread of meditation occurred historically. When meditation moved to China, where the inhabitants used words of only one syllable, the term was changed to *chan*. Later, as the practice moved to Japan, a further distortion in pronunciation altered the word to *Zen*. A direct lineage, then, can be traced from the original practice of meditation as taught in India to what may seem an entirely different practice, that of Zen. Long ago the school of meditation traveled from Kashmir to Tibet, then China and Japan; it also traveled from India to Ceylon, and throughout southeast Asia. After studying various methods of meditation, we come to the conclusion that their basic philosophy is one and the same. The Sankhya system, which is considered to be the most ancient philosophy of the world, is the philosophy behind the psychology of yoga.

Some form of meditation is practiced in each of the great religious traditions of the world. However, the practice of meditation is generally confined to the more serious and advanced students of a particular faith, and is not taught to the general public. Such advanced students, sometimes known as "mystics," are those who study most closely the original teachings of a particular faith. Meditative practices are not kept secret but are made available to all who are prepared to benefit from them. However, since most people are not disciplined, devoted or introspective enough to follow systematic meditative procedures, the deeper meditative aspects of their faith are unknown to them, and only the more superficial and outward elements are familiar.

Meditation is, of course, practiced in the Christian tradition. There is a long and well documented history of mystics who have described their meditational experiences in great detail. As our Western culture has become more secular, these practices have disappeared from the Christian religion, although there are still many Christian monks who continue in the meditative tradition.

The fact that meditation has been allied with various spiritual traditions does not necessarily mean that its practice involves following the dogma of a particular religion. Meditation is a universal experimental discipline for the development of one's consciousness, and has been experienced by the leaders of religions. The particular outward form it takes within a specific spiritual tradition reflects the beliefs and ritual of that tradition. But meditation should not be identified with the religion itself. While it can enhance one's understanding of one's faith, it can also be practiced without involvement in any religion.

All of the various methods of meditation, whether related to a specific religious belief or not, transform the mind from a state of unrest, confusion and disharmony to a state of equilibrium and joyfulness. In order to understand how this process works it will be helpful to first understand the workings of the ordinary mind. Then you will understand how meditation is a universal method for transforming the ordinary mind in order to experience abiding harmony and peace.

The Ordinary Mind

The following exercise should be tried:

Sit quietly for the next ten minutes, and think of the word "love." Keep your mind concentrated on only this single thought. Let part of your mind be an observer and watch what happens during these ten minutes of concentration. Do this exercise before reading further.

Now review your experiences during this brief exercise in concentration. You may have found that you were unable to sit comfortably for a few minutes and concentrate. Your thoughts may have turned toward your body as you became aware of physical discomforts, perhaps in your back or your legs, resulting from the way you were sitting. You may have become distracted by your breathing or have found it difficult to keep your eyes closed and relaxed. Sounds may also have disturbed you. Normally, a large variety of sensory input and physical sensations keep the mind from being able to come to rest.

Perhaps you found doubts arising in your mind and began to wonder, "What will be the outcome of this exercise?" or, "I feel foolish. Why am I doing this?" Or your mind may have been distracted by thoughts of the future, such as what you are going to do later in the day, an appointment you have, a date, some studying or work that you have left undone, or a dinner you have to prepare. Maybe you were looking forward to your next meal and thinking about how enjoyable it would be to eat, or you were worried about something that might occur later in the week.

Your mind may have wandered off to thinking of the past. For example, the word "love" may have triggered an association with some loving experiences and objects you have had in your life. These thoughts may have led you to other associations, and perhaps you created a whole drama or relived an event in your past.

Perhaps concentrating on the word "love" led you to a series of fantasies about what it might be to love another, or whether you are really capable of loving. The form of the letters in the word "love" might have attracted your attention. Some people whose imagination runs toward aesthetic images find that, in doing this exercise, they see the word before them in various colors and shapes.

Another possibility is that you were unable to concentrate on the word "love" but instead thought of exactly the opposite word, "hate."

These are the typical distractions reported by people who try this exercise: awareness of bodily sensations, concern about the future, reveries of the past, fantasies, and reactions to the object of concentration that lead to the opposite experience. If you were to do the exercise repeatedly, you would probably find that each type of thought occurred at one time or another. A large part of the teaching of meditation focuses specifically on how to deal with each of these ways in which the mind wanders, with each of these reasons and motivations for allowing the mind to drift and become uncentered. A complex teaching is necessary to help us return to the simplicity of things, to help us transcend our own complexity. It may take many years of work on various aspects of these distractions to achieve a great proficiency in meditation or in centering the mind.

When you begin to work with meditation you may think to yourself, "What have I gotten myself into? I was

doing fine until I started to meditate, but now when I sit
down and try to concentrate, my mind wanders all over the
place. There's no peace at all. It seems as if I'm going
backwards. The more I meditate the more interfering
thoughts there are." However, what is really happening is
that you are just starting to look at how your mind has
been functioning all along. When the mind is busy running
from one thing to another or when it is engaged in some
particular activity, the usual train of thoughts is kept subliminal and blocked out of awareness. For example, if you
are reading the paper in a chair, you don't notice that your
body is uncomfortable because you are so absorbed in the
thing you are doing. When you are adding numbers to
figure up an account, because of the mind's active involvement, the preconscious or unconscious associations remain
in the background, outside of awareness. It is only when
you try to bring your mind to a more restful state that you
begin to notice the subtle tensions in your body and the
vast, unending stream of associated thoughts. You may
have been quite surprised during the concentration exercise
to find an abundance of reveries, worries, concerns, and
distractions in your mind.

The ordinary mind and thinking process might be
characterized as a turbulent lake, with the surface an endless
flow of waves. It is this constant stream of concerns, hopes,
fears, and anxieties coming before your mind that leads you
to experience a state of restlessness and unhappiness.
Psychologists have called the flow of one's thoughts, a chain
of associations. The first thought triggers another which is
associated with still another, so that a whole chain of

interlocked thoughts constantly flows through your mind, leading it hither and thither. In this process of constantly moving from one thought to another, you are left bewildered and your energy and awareness are scattered.

The first stage of meditation involves becoming aware of your distracted and chaotic state of mind. Once you do this, you are able to begin correcting your deficiencies. Thoughts put into your subconscious mind are like dust swept under a rug. They do not really go away. You have no control over them, yet the train of associations they trigger still affects your behavior. The process of meditation is similar to that process of psychotherapy in that it brings impressions which ordinarily remain in the unconscious to the conscious mind so that they may be brought under scrutiny and may then be controlled. Thus you can decide how realistic a fear or worry or expectation is and dismiss it if you choose. You can decide consciously how to act instead of reacting blindly on the basis of thoughts which remain buried in your unconscious. Once the thoughts come into your consciousness they no longer carry an impelling driven quality. Those thoughts which are not helpful to you can then be dismissed from your mind entirely. The process of meditation involves first becoming aware of the associative train of thoughts and then learning how to dismiss it instead of becoming carried away by them. As the turbulent thoughts are released, the mind and body are calmed. Eventually, the inherent state of peace and joy within shines forth into experience. There is no other way to reach a deeper state of awareness except by the centering of meditation in one form or another, and there is no other way to find abiding happiness.

Once in a great while we have all experienced a state of
mind different from the usual, in which suddenly we seem
to feel very peaceful. For a few moments our cares and
concerns may drop away and we find ourselves at one with
the present. A sense of peace, a sense of being at home,
comes over us during this brief pause in the frenzy of our
mental functioning. This experience may feel like moving
from the turbulence of a hurricane to the center where there
is a state of calm. Or it might be compared to diving below
the stormy surface of the ocean to find peace and stillness
in the depths below. You have perhaps experienced a rare
moment such as this when playing with children or being out
in the country. We often seek to return to this sort of
experience but do not know the way. Meditation is a
method that leads the mind to that center of calm and joy
which is similar to the state that sometimes may be experienced spontaneously.

What Causes the Mind to be Restless?

If you look closely at the various fears, hopes, expectations and thoughts that pass through your mind, you can
trace them back to one source. In every case, the turbulence
of the mind is based upon the various desires that you
have. When you are content, at that moment there are no
desires in the mind. But the moment a desire arises, you
become discontented because you find yourself separated
from the source of satisfaction. Satisfaction is attained
when you fulfill the desire or achieve a unity in which the
source of satisfaction is no longer separate from you.

Imagine yourself sitting without any thought in your

mind. Suddenly a thought comes along: "I am hungry," or, "I want to call my friends," or, "I wish I hadn't said what I did this morning." Most of the thoughts which appear before your mind are based upon a desire or upon some imbalance which is experienced. This gives rise to a need to set things right or do something to put things back into harmony again. Those thoughts which spring from disharmony and dissatisfaction lead the mind from peacefulness. Meditation is a process of systematically replacing thoughts arising from desires, longings and dissatisfactions, with thoughts of harmony and contentment.

We all want to experience joy; we all want to feel peace. If you ask a number of people what they want from life, almost everyone will say that they wish happiness, joy and peace for themselves as well as for others. One person might say, "I want to be content." Someone else may say, "I want to feel peaceful," another, "One time I had this really joyful feeling, this exuberance. I would really like to feel that again." These are really all variants of the same thing, that is, the wish to be in a state where we have what we desire, where there are no dissatisfactions. Many people feel that this is an ideal, an unobtainable state and that the very nature of human life precludes any continuous state of joy, peace and satisfaction. However, it is possible to maintain a state of joy and harmony through the practice of meditation.

The way in which you've tried to find peace and satisfaction is to look for objects in the world which promise that experience. So you might say, "Wow! I really had a great feeling when I was out sailing one time. I just felt so much in harmony. I'm going to buy a sailboat and go sailing every weekend, as I want to experience that joy again." So you buy a sailboat to recapture that wonderful experience. But more often than not, you will find that that unique moment cannot be relived. Although sailing is often enjoyable, it doesn't provide that abiding joy you are seeking. Instead it brings many displeasures such as transporting your boat, repairing it, and working to pay for it, which take more time than you spend in sailing. The boat may eventually become such a burden that you sell it and look for a new object to bring you happiness. Perhaps your friends have told you that skiing or camping is an exhilarating experience, so you think about investing in some new gear. Again and again you become attracted by these alluring experiences, often to turn away from them in disappointment after a brief flirtation. You come to believe that all happiness is indeed temporary and elusive.

Sometimes we seek to find happiness by creating the "right" external situation. Some people will look for happiness in having a large and comfortable house. Other people think, "If only I could live in the woods. I can't be happy here. There's all this traffic noise and people are always bothering me. If I could get a nice cabin in the country and be with nature I'd be really happy."

Concentrating on the external objects of the world is not the purpose of meditation. Meditation helps one know one's own internal aspects, and finally leads one to the source of consciousness. This inward process requires a thorough training of body, senses and mind. If these three are not properly trained, the aim of meditation is hardly achieved; you can meditate for years and not attain the goal.

Yoga psychology offers a systematic method of training

all aspects of our functioning. There are six preliminary steps recommended in yoga psychology to prepare one for the seventh step which is called meditation. If these steps are properly understood, they help a student have control over those thoughts which are helpful and reject those thoughts which are not helpful.

The *yamas* and *niyamas* (ten guides to living) have their essential value in helping attain the purpose of meditation. Without practicing them one cannot communicate with the people one lives with; nor can one have a balanced, tranquil mind. Since an unhealthy body can also become a source of distraction and an obstacle, it is helpful to work with it as a preliminary to meditation. A still, steady and comfortable posture should be practiced. A harmonious deep, even breath is equally necessary. The habit of steadying the mind with all its subtleties is very important. When one practices meditation systematically, one will find that concentration is the most important factor in attaining *samadhi*. If a dissipated mind is led towards the object of meditation, instead of experiencing peace, it will start hallucinating or going toward passive, drowsy states. When concentration is strengthened and starts flowing one-pointedly, it becomes meditation. The finest state of meditation is called *samadhi*. In this state a unique experience of oneness is attained.

The need for meditation arises because: (1) all of our methods of learning and teaching are based on external objects; (2) we do not know the totality of ourselves; (3) we consider the learning we acquire through books to be sufficient for enlightenment, when actually direct experience alone is valid; all other resources are only means; (4) truth lies within, and the process of meditation alone helps us to realize the truth; (5) relationships in the external world cannot be understood without understanding life within. Meditation can help us in each of these areas. If yoga psychology is thoroughly practiced, it leads us to proper solution of our various problems.

If we look more closely at the process of searching for happiness in objects or situations outside of ourselves, we will see that it is extremely inefficient and self-defeating for two important reasons:

1. Seeking happiness in external objects leads to small momentary islands of satisfaction in the midst of a preponderance of restlessness.

There is, of course, the momentary satisfaction of achieving one's goal or of possessing the object that is desired. This satisfaction creates the illusion that joy resides in the objects which fulfill desires. If you are hungry and have an ice cream cone that is enjoyable, you tend to believe that the ice cream cone made you feel good. In this way you create a list in your mind of objects which are satisfying, objects which "make you feel happy." You also create a list of experiences or objects which lead to unhappiness and are to be avoided. These lists form a greater part of the thoughts and associations coming into your consciousness. Whenever there is a lull in your directed activity, a thought from one of these two lists is likely to come to your conscious attention. The appearance of this thought will most likely lead to your going off in the direction of seeking satisfaction in or avoiding the object you have thought of.

Thinking of your desires and aversions creates a state of almost constant restlessness in your mental functioning.

The objects of desire satisfy only temporarily. Soon after the ice cream cone is eaten and you feel satisfied and contented, your mind will begin to search for another object of satisfaction. You think, "What should I do now? Maybe I should go to the movies." Once again, you feel a desire and fulfill it. When it is fulfilled, another momentary satisfaction is realized, only for you to again become dissatisfied and seek something new. In this way your mind is kept constantly busy and your whole life is consumed in the process of pursuing one satisfaction, temporarily feeling good, and then pursuing another. You find little islands of enjoyment in the midst of worry, confusion and agitation.

2. The source of happiness does not really reside in the objects attained but in a state of mind which is independent of these objects.

The way in which objects are mistaken to be the source of happiness is made clear by the following analogy. Imagine yourself in a dark room with a flashlight. Without the light you can see nothing, but when the light from the flashlight falls on an object, that object is illuminated. First the light falls on a jewel. As it is reflected off the jewel toward you, it takes on the green color of an emerald, a particular shape and quality of hardness and solidity. The light as it is reflected by the emerald is quite different from the original light, and it may give you a certain satisfaction, causing you to exclaim, "How beautiful it is. I enjoy gazing at it."

Now, the light moves from the emerald and is focused

upon an attractive person and comes back to you to create
a feeling of tenderness. This is an entirely different experience, though the same light source illuminates both objects.
Originally, the light is pure and has no form. As it falls upon
a whole series of objects, each one "packages" the light in a
particular way. Each object transmutes or distorts the light
from its original state, giving it a certain coloration and
reflecting back only particular qualities and only a portion of
the total energy. One object may lead you to feel a sense of
status and importance; another object may be a source of
sexual gratification; an object of food may lead you to
another kind of pleasure. The light itself is unlimited in its
ability to illumine all of the different objects. Each single
object, however, is able to reflect only its particular form,
and without the light source it would not be experienced.

From this analogy, we might say that all of the various
satisfactions we experience in the world are reflections of this
pure energy. The light is diluted, given a certain form, tied
with a special ribbon and then handed back to you. If you
were to forget about the source of light and believe that
the illumination was coming from the object itself, you
might then believe that it is the form which is creating the
experience of pleasure or aversion. You might easily become
attached to that form so that when the form was no longer
there you would feel distressed.

However, if you detach your attention enough from the
object of your desire to see that the object is reflecting light
from another source, if you begin to realize that your own
light is the illumination, then you will also recognize that the
source of experience remains even when the object is no
longer being focused upon. The process of meditation is

exactly that of following the light to its source. Attention is gradually withdrawn from the object and traced back toward this source of illumination, so that the energy can be experienced in its unalloyed, intense form. As the mind is brought toward this source in its pure state, less energy is spent in seeking union with those external things identified as objects of satisfaction. Meditation teaches us that there is a source of joy, peace and happiness already abiding within. It is as if the light we have been describing is at the center of your own being.

This center of energy is our true nature or inner Self. Just as the light in the dark room illuminates various objects, giving them form and color, so does the inner light of our true nature illumine our minds, bodies and senses. The world outside is shaped by our five senses and exists insofar as it is a reflection of the inner light. We are drawn outwards by our senses and distracted by these reflections to such a degree that we forget the very existence of the inner light from which has arisen all of these reflections. We falsely identify with our egos, minds, bodies and senses, forgetting our true nature which is beyond all of this and from which all of this has arisen. Man is truly immortal but through this false identification chooses to be mortal. The ego, mind and body are subject to death and decay, but the inner light is without beginning or end. Meditation first makes us aware of this inner light and then leads us to complete identification with our true nature. We will then see things in their true perspective. We will see that the same inner light shines in all of us and that we are all a part of the same universal consciousness just as the drops of water that form an ocean share all of the qualities of the ocean. This is the state of *samadhi*, or

expanded, all-encompassing consciousness, the goal of
meditation. With this realization will come the emergence
from the narrow confines of the senses, body, mind and ego
to a state of universal consciousness—a state of divinity in
which human imperfections and limitations are transcended.

If your energy is scattered and dissipated over a variety
of objects which give you pleasure, the pleasurable experience can only be as great as each investment of energy. You
listen to a record, go to the movies, spend time with a friend,
etc., but each experience only partially reflects the intensity
of the original light. But when the energy is collected back
to its center, the place from which it originates, it is greatly
intensified, much in the way an ordinary light beam is
focused into a laser beam. As a result of this focusing of
energy, the laser beam is tremendously useful in ways
impossible, were the energy scattered. Similarly, a magnifying
glass can burn a hole in a piece of paper by concentrating the
diffuse sunlight.

Our energy within, when properly focused, leads to
experiences which have more satisfaction than any variety
of objects can bring. If you could experience this light
itself, you would begin to find greater pleasure within yourself, and objects would no longer be needed in the same way.
The highest states of meditation, as described by those who
have experienced them, that is, those who have been able to
follow the light to its source with undivided attention, are
states of ever-new bliss and unbounded joy.

Many people feel that without objects to strive after,
we would be in a state of emptiness or boredom. This
misconception is based upon viewing objects as the source of
gratification in the world. The person who becomes bored

is very much attached to objects. His mind is still focused outwardly and he believes that finding an object leads to gratification. His boredom stems from the fact that he does not have an object for which to strive at that particular moment. Boredom comes from wanting an object and yet not having one. The person who is bored has not the realization that joy can be experienced without objects. He makes no effort to turn the attention within to this joy. The Meditator, by contrast, has freed his mind from craving an object and he allows himself to experience internal joy and peace. He cannot possibly experience boredom.

Withdrawal versus Involvement

The analogy of following a light back to its source may have suggested to you that you should withdraw all your attention from outward experiences. However, the explanation of this process is still incomplete. Although it seems paradoxical, meditation may lead you to become more active and effective in the world.

A certain amount of time is spent alone in the practice of meditation. But this can be compared to the time spent alone learning anything, whether it be yoga, chemistry, or playing the violin. If you decided to play the violin, you would have to get a teacher, perhaps go to him each week, and then continue your practice between lessons. The amount of time you would spend withdrawing from your other worldly activities and sitting by yourself in a room to practice would be a function of the seriousness of purpose. It could be fifteen minutes or several hours each day. Likewise, in order to make progress in meditation, time must be invested in practice, whether you are a beginner or a very advanced student.

When you understand the meditative process more completely, you will realize that there is really a change in attitude while relating to the world rather than an actual disengagement from activity. This is often misunderstood, as illustrated by the story of two monks who approached a small river. A young woman who was waiting there asked them to help her across. The first monk did not respond, but the second carried her across. As they continued on their way, the first monk was very upset and said, "You know we're not supposed to associate with women." Whereupon the second replied, "I put her down on the riverbank but I see that you are still carrying her."

As you become more aware of your own center through meditation, you will withdraw from *dependence* on objects and people as sources of gratification. This does not imply that you will no longer enjoy experiences of being with others. Instead it means that you will not look for satisfaction, comfort and stability from others. You will not put unrealisitc demands on others which they cannot possibly fulfill; rather you will be free to relate from your sense of completeness. As you become aware of the source of joy within, you will spontaneously begin to share your abundance with others.

Being under the influence of your desires distorts and limits your ability to relate to others. When you are dependent on people and objects for your source of pleasure, your whole vision becomes colored. For example, if you are a person who is predominantly influenced by lustful desires, you will tend to relate to each new person of the opposite sex you meet as an object to satisfy you. Your whole vision will be narrowed by that perspective, and you will tend to neglect all the other qualities which people have.

The practice of meditation leads to enriched relationships with other people. Seeing people less as objects to satisfy your desires allows you to notice things about them which previously went unobserved. Instead of trying to get something from your relationships, whether it be money, sex, a delicious meal, or security, your satisfaction and contentment will rest in yourself, and you will be free to relate to people in a very natural way, enjoying whatever qualities they may wish to share with you. You will be more interested in what you can give to your friends than in what they can do for you. And with the realization that love is something which radiates out from a fullness within, "I need you" will change to "I love you."

In order for us to develop together it is necessary for those who feel calm and centered inside to help the many people today who are in a state of conflict. You cannot do this if you withdraw and sit somewhere by yourself. As people become involved in the meditational experience, they become more sensitive to what there is to do in the world. At the same time, their own capacities are developed to such an extent that other people begin seeking what they have to offer. The misconception that the perfect yogi lives all alone in a cave where he sits all day in quiet meditation is quite common in the West. It is an escapist fantasy, however, to imagine that this is really all a yogi does.

II

How to Practice Meditation

The following guidelines will help you in your practice of meditation. Try to follow them systematically. If you return to this chapter after you've been practicing for some time, you'll find suggestions that were overlooked in your first reading, and you can readjust your practice accordingly.

Choosing a Place

Choose a place of meditation which you will use regularly, rather than move from one place to another each time you meditate. This will create a certain atmosphere, expectations and feelings around this particular spot for meditation, and will accentuate the positive effect of your meditation experience.

In order to choose a spot for your meditation it is suggested that you walk about your room, apartment, or house and pick a place that feels comfortable to you. It should be a place that is quiet and free from distractions. Your meditation place should not be overly warm so that you become drowsy; rather it should be slightly cool and well-ventilated so that your mind can remain alert. Meditation is best done without the distractions of stimuli such as sound and light. You will notice a distinct calming effect in your meditation at night if you turn the lights off.

The spot should be such that you can face either East or North, since you are subtly affected by the polarity of the magnetic fields of the earth. Facing south during meditation will have a negative effect on your mental functioning, while facing East or North will create a positive effect. These effects are sutble and unconscious. One of the French doctors has done extensive experimentation on this subject.

How to Sit

You may sit in a straight-back chair for meditation or on the floor in one of the traditional postures, with legs crossed. If you choose to sit on the floor, place a soft wool blanket, folded into quarters, on your meditation spot. . Do not lie down to meditate, for you will tend to doze off.

If you sit directly on the floor, you may find that after a short period of time your back feels uncomfortable, and you have a tendency to lean forward. This produces a noticeable curvature in your back. It is important in meditation to sit with the spine straight and head erect.

This injunction is emphasized by all schools of meditation, as it leads to a harmonizing of the breath, the nervous system and the mind. The nervous system coordinates the functions of all other systems of the body. It consists of the central or voluntary nervous system and the autonomic or involuntary nervous system, further subdivided into the parasympathetic and sympathetic systems which regulate "involuntary" functions such as the beating of the heart, the secretion of digestive organs, etc. The spinal cord forms a major portion of the central nervous system, being in a sense, a prolongation of the brain. The sympathetic system consists mainly of two nerve cell clusters of gangliated chords lying on either side of the spinal cord. The parasympathetic system consists mainly of the vagus nerve or south cranial nerve which also travels along the spinal cord. The position of the spinal cord is, therefore, important in terms of the workings of the nervous system. Keeping the head, neck and trunk erect allows the spinal cord to assume its natural, graceful S-shaped contour. This natural position is essential for the flow of subtler energies through the spinal cord, which governs the workings of the mind. This emphasis on posture is also related to the breath in that it allows deep, smooth and complete inhalation and exhalation. The posture is, therefore, important in harmonizing the breathing and the energies of the nervous system, this harmony leading to a calmer state of mind.

Most westerners who have not become accustomed to sitting on the floor in a cross-legged position cannot maintain the straightness of the spine. However, if you sit on a *firm* pillow, or a second blanket folded several times, your buttocks will be raised a few inches above the floor and you will find that it is more comfortable to sit this way and much easier to keep your spine straight. This will make the difference between an agonizing period of meditation and a comfortable and enjoyable experience. Some beginners find it helpful to sit with their backs against the wall. This may be done initially. As the muscles of your back become stronger, however, it is suggested that you move away from the wall for a brief period of time as you sit to meditate, and gradually increase this time until you can sit with your spine free throughout your meditation.

Sitting upon a cushion on the floor, you may cross your legs so that the ankle of each foot is just below the opposite knee. This position has traditionally been known as the "easy" or "comfortable pose" for meditation. You may find that your legs "fall asleep" after a few minutes of sitting this way. This is caused by your foot pressing against the main artery of the opposite leg, so that the blood flow is reduced. You need not be concerned about this, and if it is not unduly uncomfortable, you may continue to meditate. However, be sure to carefully come out of this position at the end of the meditation and allow the normal circulation to return before you attempt to stand up and move about.

If you find sitting on the floor uncomfortable, you may sit upright in a straight-back chair. There is nothing magical or especially beneficial about sitting on the floor in the initial stages, and you may make greater progress by choosing a chair instead. The chair should be firm so that you may sit upright and do not slouch. If possible, sit with your back free, that is, not touching the back of the chair, and rest your feet flat on the floor.

In either the sitting position on the floor or in a chair, rest your hands comfortably on your knees or in your lap. If you place your hands in your lap, turn them so that the palms are facing upwards and the right hand is resting in the left palm.

The purpose of sitting in an easy, comfortable and steady posture is to make the mind steady, one-pointed and free of distractions. Once you have chosen a comfortable position for meditation, remain still in that position throughout your meditation period, rather than squirming about or adjusting your posture.

You may wish to wrap yourself in a blanket or shawl at the start of your meditation. There is a tendency for the metabolic processes to slow down as you meditate and you may find yourself becoming cool.

The Time of Meditation

It is helpful to have a particular time for meditation which can be regularly adhered to. Your mind and body will become accustomed to meditating at your chosen time and it will be easier for you to go deeper into the meditative state. Choosing a particular place and a particular time are very important to the meditation process. This cannot be over-emphasized.

As a beginning student, it is suggested that you meditate twice a day for approximately twenty minutes. After a few weeks you may increase the time to thirty minutes at each sitting. You may increase the time further as you desire, eventually sitting for an hour, or increase the number of meditations per day from two to four. However, do not force yourself to sit for a longer time or to meditate more frequently. If the time is increased, it should be a natural and spontaneous occurrence because of the joy and pleasure found in meditation.

Do not be too quick to adopt what you may think of as a "meditative life style." Those who make the most sudden and drastic changes in their habits and life style typically do not continue in their practice. After a few weeks or a few months, having exhausted themselves by trying a new way of life, they take a brief rest and move on to a new fad or temporary solution to their plight. Gradual day-by-day growth will, in the long run, prove far more beneficial.

Set aside at least two times each day when you can regularly be alone, when there is quiet about you, and when you will not be disturbed. If you have a family, you may choose to rise before everyone else or to go to bed later. The best times for meditation are upon awakening in the morning and before retiring at night. During the early morning and late night hours when others are sleeping, there is usually a quietness about and the mood is conducive to meditation. Sunrise and sunset are also auspicious times for meditation. During these times of the day there is a particular calm and tranquility which affects the meditative experience. The hour before noon and between five and six o'clock in the evening are also considered to be favorable times for meditation. Since meditation is best done when your stomach is empty and energy is not being taken up in digestion, the period just before your meals may also be selected. Do not meditate after eating. You are likely to feel sluggish and your mind is dulled after a meal as energy is being channeled to the digestive organs.

If you chronically find yourself becoming drowsy during meditation, you may precede your meditation with some yoga postures. These will make you feel more alert and will allow you to sit comfortably for a much longer period of time.

You may be concerned about the amount of time that is needed to meditate regularly and may feel that it is not possible for you to get up earlier and go to bed later at night.

However, as you practice meditation, hatha yoga (physical postures) or pranayama (breathing exercises), you are likely to find that you will need less sleep each night. Much of the psychological benefit from the dream stage of sleep is gained during meditation. One function of this stage of sleep is to resolve conflicts in the mind which are unsettled from the day before. Meditation accomplishes much the same work since many of the distracting thoughts that come before your mind in meditation are based on the conflicts of the day. As you learn to neutralize these conflicts in meditation, you are accomplishing a great deal of the work of dream sleep, and so fewer hours of sleep each night are needed. The rejuvenating effect of hatha yoga postures and pranayama will similarly reduce your need for sleep. It is not uncommon for students to find their need for sleep reduced by the same amount as they spend in these practices each day. So that if they were formerly sleeping eight hours each night and now spend two hours in meditation and other yogic practices, they often find their need for sleep is reduced to about six hours. Each individual is different and this may not be true in your case. However, after you have been meditating for a few weeks, you might try reducing your sleep and see the effect this has upon you.

Gradually as meditation becomes more central in your life, your schedule will rearrange itself. In time, many activities which lead to unrest will fall away. They will no longer seem to be much fun. Instead of seeking out activities which involved disturbance, confusion and restlessness, you will forego these activities and free an abundance of time for more peaceful and harmonious experiences.

Preparation for Meditation

Meditation should not be undertaken in a haphazard way. If you come from a rush of activity, immediately sit down and start meditating, you will find that your mind is very distracted. Your anxieties related to earlier experiences that day may carry over into your meditation and you may be unable to calm down at all. Therefore, preliminary relaxation and breathing exercises are practiced before each meditation to calm the mind and prepare it for meditation itself.

When you come from whatever activity you have been doing and take your meditation seat, the first thing you must do is create the proper attitude for yourself. Decide that during this meditational experience, nothing will disturb you. Put aside all worries about things that have occurred before, of things that are still to be completed in the future. Have the attitude, "I'm going to take these twenty minutes from all of the cares I have. My concerns will be dealt with later at the proper time and in the proper manner. But for this short period of time my meditation is *the most important thing* and nothing else will take precedence over it."

Having decided that meditation is more important than anything else for the moment, you are now ready for some purifying exercises and for the systematic relaxation of all of the muscles in your body.

Breathing and Relaxation

The flow of your breath has a close relationship to your mental state. When you are emotional, upset, or anxious, your breath becomes irregular. When you are calm, your breath is smooth and even. These breathing exercises are recommended since they bring your mind to a peaceful yet alert state, by giving an internal cleansing to your respiratory system. They empty your lungs of carbon dioxide and bring an abundant supply of oxygen. They will purify the nervous system and leave you with a feeling of freshness and purity. The exercises are to be done after you sit comfortably on your meditation seat and before you begin meditation.

First Breathing Exercise: *The Complete Breath*

Exhale completely and slowly. Inhale for a count of sixteen (or to your capacity with straining). Immediately begin a slow exhalation for exactly the same count as your inhalation. Breathe only through your nostrils, not from your mouth. Try to use your diaphragm and stomach muscles in breathing and not just the rib cage and shoulders. Continue for three to seven repetitions of the "complete breath."

Second Exercise: *Alternate Nostril Breathing*

Place your right hand so that your index and middle fingers are resting at the space between your two eyebrows. Rest your ring and little finger gently against your left nostril near the lower edge. Place your thumb on your right nostril near the lower edge.

Press your thumb against the right nostril so that the nostril is blocked and exhale slowly from the open left nostril only, counting to six as you exhale. Immediately inhale through the same left nostril for a count of six.

This exhalation and inhalation makes up one round. Repeat for two more rounds with the left nostril open.

After the third inhalation, close the left nostril with your little and ring fingers and open the right nostril, exhaling for six seconds and then inhaling through the same nostril. Repeat two more rounds through the open right nostril. (With practice you may increase the count of each inhalation and exhalation up to sixteen seconds. However, the time span for exhalation and inhalation should always be equal and should remain unchanged within one practice session).

After three rounds of this "alternate breathing" through each nostril, bring your hand down and slowly resume the normal rhythm of your breath. Become aware of the breath flowing evenly through both nostrils. If one nostril is blocked, you may wish to repeat the exercise. When the breath is flowing equally through both nostrils, you will find that you become calm and joyful.

Relaxation Exercise

When you have completed the breathing exercise, it will be helpful to relax the various muscles in your body. Mental tension is often correlated with tension in the body. Systematic relaxation of the musculature will lead to a calmer state of mind. It will free energy which is being used to hold the body rigid, will allow you to sit in meditation for a longer period of time in greater comfort and ease, and will allow you to rest your attention more completely on your chosen object of meditation.

In order to relax your body, bring your attention to a set of muscles and mentally ask those muscles to relax. Then feel the muscles following your direction and becoming limp. Slowly relax the muscles in the parts of your body in the order given: *forehead, eyebrows, eyes, cheeks, jaw, throat, shoulders, upper arms, forearms, wrists, hands, fingers, chest, stomach, hips, thighs, calves, ankles, feet, toes.*

Relax each set of muscles as completely as possible while keeping the spine straight and head erect. When you have completed this relaxation, you may proceed to meditate.

The first time you attempt this relaxation exercise, you may have little awareness or control over the tension or relaxation in these muscles. You may notice very little effect. Do not become discouraged. After following this procedure for several times, you will begin to enjoy its soothing, calming effect.

Methods of Meditation

It is not possible to center your mind by simply saying, "I'm going to have a blank, empty mind, free of worries and concerns." Your mind will seek out some thought upon which to focus attention and will jump from one idea to another in rapid succession. All of the meditative traditions seek to counter this tendency by giving the mind one simple thought upon which it may be centered. By having a steady focus, all of the distracting thoughts eventually fade into the background. The various meditative traditions are fundamentally the same except that they use different thoughts or objects as the device for centering. Almost all meditative traditions use a particular thought, a particular prayer or chant, as a focus so that the mind may collect itself. It is only through this recollective (re-collective) process that it is possible to expand your awareness and to achieve the higher states of consciousness which are variously described as *samadhi*, Christ-consciousness or *nirvana*.

We will explore three meditative methods so that you can experience the various effects of having different objects upon which to center your mind.

Centering on Sounds:
A Preliminary Tibetan Method of Meditation

As you sit calmly with your eyes closed and your spine erect, become aware of the sounds you hear. These sounds may be the sounds from the room, the sounds outside, such as traffic noises, or the sounds from your own internal bodily functions. Bring your attention and awareness to whatever sounds there are to be heard. After a few minutes of sitting in this way, become aware not only of sounds but also the space between the sounds. As you hear sounds from various sources, you will experience a sense of three dimensional space with soundless or empty spaces in the midst of sound sources. You will also notice an interval of time between one sound and another during which there is relative silence. Let your mind rest on the experience of both sound and its absence.

This is a traditional Tibetan meditational method used for beginners to help them become aware of the emptiness which underlies form. It is an excellent method for beginning students because it allows the mind to focus on an object undergoing change. Since the object of concentration has variety rather than steadiness, it is easier for the beginner to remain interested. After meditating with this method for several days or a few weeks, it will be helpful to choose an object which is more steady and internal. You may then begin to practice meditation on the breath for a similar period of time.

Meditation on Breath: A traditional Buddhist Meditation

Close your eyes and begin to be aware of the natural rhythm of your breathing. Sit for several minutes watching your breath, without attempting to control it in any way. Allow your breathing to become more effortless. As you watch your breath and relax, its pattern may change. It may become more slow and even.

After some time, focus your attention on the area just below the rib cage in the front center of your body. You may notice that as you inhale the muscles below the ribs in the navel area tend to move outwards slightly, and as you exhale the stomach area slightly contracts. This movement is caused by the motion of the muscle just below the lungs, which is called the diaphragm. When the air is taken in, this muscle contracts into a flat shape, allowing the lungs to expand downward and the lower lungs to be filled with air. When the lungs are full, this muscle lies flat, like a pancake. Then, as the air is expelled, the muscle relaxes and moves upward into a dome shape, forcing the air out of the lower lungs. The stomach moves out slightly, as the diaphragm flattens with inhalation and it moves in with the exhalation.

In this meditational technique, rest your attention on

the movement of the diaphragm. Become sensitive to it by simply concentrating on this area. As you inhale, bring to mind the thought "falling" and as you exhale the thought "rising." Simply watch the rise and fall of this muscle along with the flow of the breath. At first it may be difficult to be sensitive to this movement. You may notice the movement of the stomach area in and out rather than the rising and falling movement. However, with time and patience, your sensitivity will increase so that you will become more aware of the diaphragm moving. As you allow yourself to breathe with the proper movement of the diaphragm, you will feel a deep sense of peace.

The breath is the connecting link between you and your environment. A great portion of the nourishment that you take comes in through the breath. Without breath there is no life. Focusing your attention on breathing in this way subtly makes you aware of this intimate connection between what you think of as "I" and the nurturing force about you. In time, the distinction between the two may be dissolved. Instead of putting any effort into breathing for yourself, watch your breath with the attitude that you are being breathed.

Many meditative traditions teach that breath and mind are so coordinated that it is impossible to separate the two. As your attention becomes more keenly aware of the breathing process, *without attempting to control it*, the breathing will become more rhythmical, more finely attuned, and with this, the mind will become more calm and centered.

After working with this meditation for some time, you may go on to the next practice, which includes the use of sound along with breath.

Meditation with Mantra

In yoga meditation and in several other meditative traditions, a sound or word is used as the object of meditation. Sometimes the word, or *mantra* as it is called in the Eastern traditions, is spoken aloud, but usually it is repeated mentally.*

A traditional mantra used in yoga meditation is *so-hum* which may be translated "I am that." To use this mantra in your meditation, sit with your back straight and eyes closed. Allow your attention to rest on your breath for a few minutes, as you have been instructed to do in the previous exercise. Then begin to remember the mantra *so-hum* in harmony with the natural rhythm of your breath. As you inhale, allow the word *so* (translated "that") to come into your awareness, and as you exhale, remember *hum* (translated "I am"). Do not make an effort to repeat this sound. Simply observe the sound as it comes into your consciousness. The sounds *so* and *hum* are, in fact, the natural sounds made during the inbreath and outbreath respectively.

The Progressive Use of Meditational Techniques

When you are working with one meditation method, be consistent. Do not give in to the temptation of choosing one method one day and another the next or of changing methods in the midst of a meditation because your meditation

---

* The significance of mantra will be explained in some detail in the next chapter. For now, only practical guidance in using mantra meditation will be given.

does not seem to be going well. Meditation is a process to unify your scattered mind. To jump from one method to another will only create more uncertainty and confusion.

Progressing from one properly used technique to another after a few weeks will allow you to move gradually into more advanced and more focused centering. Do not judge the efficacy of one method over another by what seems the most peaceful or easy in your initial experiences. The meditation technique which seems most difficult at first may, once you have assimilated it, be more helpful to you than a method that you prefer initially.

After practicing meditation on sounds and then on breath for some time, it is suggested that you continue to practice the *so-hum* method of meditation. When you have formed a habit of daily meditations and a sincere commitment to continuing your practice and development, it may be your wish to proceed to the next step: receiving a personal mantra directly from a qualified teacher of meditation. You will then have a center of concentration which is chosen to suit your own unique personality and developmental needs, as well as the personal guidance of an established meditative tradition.

The Meditation Experience: How to Deal with Disturbing Thoughts

The process of meditation is a means of working out the conflicts in your mind, and learning how to deal with potentially disturbing thoughts so that they lose their unsettling, upsetting effect. The way you relate to troublesome thoughts in meditation is the critical and central aspect of the meditative process. Without understanding how to do this properly, superficially concentrating on the breath or repeating a mantra will accomplish little. The whole process of meditation is nothing but the practical study of how to deal with disturbing thoughts. There are some guidelines for this practice which will be of great help. When you learn the proper way of relating to distracting thoughts, you will achieve great peace and serenity.

Even these disturbing thoughts are helpful in the long run. They rise from the unconscious to conscious awareness. As such, they increase your awareness, that is, they expand your conscious mind and diminish disturbance in the unconscious mind.

Do not feel that when you have a pleasant experience you are having a "good" meditation and when you have a lot of intrusions disrupting your concentration you are having a "bad" meditation. Because even the intrusions may be helpful to you. A restless meditation, in fact, may be more helpful than one which is pleasant.

Meditation is not only a calming process, but is also a process of consciousness-expansion. The thoughts which are buried in your subconscious mind are coming forward during meditation, and you are becoming aware of them. When upsetting or distracting thoughts remain in the unconscious they lead to disturbances in your functioning, to feelings of anxiety, and to seemingly irrational behavior. You are not in control of these thoughts or your responses to them. However, when you allow unsettling thoughts to come to the surface, you are no longer a slave to them, reacting without awareness. The fact that they come into your awareness means that they are losing their power over you as motivating forces. They now become subject to your conscious, volitional control.

When these thoughts express themselves, an emptying process occurs. Rather than maintaining them in the vast reservoir of the unconscious, they burst like bubbles which have come to the surface of a lake. They are no longer retained. During the meditation process your mind is slowly being emptied of accumulated, unsettling forces. The meditator works much like a sculptor, removing the excess material so that what lies hidden may be revealed. In this case, the excess of collected worries, concerns and fantasies is slowly being discarded to reveal a hidden treasure of joy.

You may carry over your tendency to set goals for yourself into your meditation practice. Even students who have been practicing meditation for some time have difficulty in leaving this tendency.

There will be a tendency again and again to set expectations for yourself and to try to meet those expectations, to judge your performance and to give yourself either a star or a black mark. It will be much more useful to regard whatever you experience in meditation as helpful rather than having the idea of *trying* to achieve anything in particular. Once you have learned not to try in meditation, you will truly have accomplished something. The experience should not be forced in any way. If you *try* to achieve any particular goal in meditation, you will inevitably experience a great deal of frustration, and you will not have pleasant experiences.

Researchers who have been studying control over the internal processes have found that exerting too much effort in trying to achieve control in this area does not lead to successful results and in fact may lead to just the opposite of the desired experience. These Western researchers, working with bio-feedback, are discovering techniques of self-control similar to those which were developed by Eastern meditative traditions thousands of years ago.

They are finding out, for example, that if one wishes to slow his heart or produce certain kinds of brain waves indicative of a peaceful state of mind, the more the student tries to achieve this state, the more impossible it becomes. It is only when an attitude of what has been termed "passive volition" is adopted that success is achieved. Passive volition involves an attitude of letting it happen, of just observing things rather than trying to gain active control over what is happening. Many students working with the control of physiological functioning find that it is only when they "give up" that real change begins to take place.

In meditation there is, of course, a given object of concentration which creates a frame of reference. The mind is not drifting aimlessly. Within this framework, however, there should not be a strong effort to maintain focus on that object. Instead, the attitude should be to simply witness how the mind rests on the object of concentration. As you do this, you will find that your mind will very frequently wander off to other objects, other thoughts. It is at this point that the idea of not trying becomes important. If you can simply maintain a natural observing attitude, or what the Buddhists call "bare attention," you will no doubt find that the distracting thoughts will slowly diminish and eventually disappear of themselves. You will then experience the deepest state of meditation.

As a beginner, however, you will find a tendency to

relate to distracting thoughts in the same way as you deal with disturbances in your everyday life. Accordingly, you will make one of two mistakes generally made in the meditative process. If your everyday attitude and behavior is more passive and you go along with whatever comes your way, you will tend to become absorbed in the thoughts which distract your mind and you will be carried away from your meditational center. If, on the other hand, you are usually argumentative and often engage yourself in conflicts, you may try to force disturbing thoughts from your mind when meditating. Although either of these may be a predominant tendency for you, you will find that both ways of dealing with random thoughts will occur.

The process of meditation, when properly learned, creates a third alternative way of dealing with distracting thoughts. Rather than react to certain thoughts as positive and become absorbed in or identify with them, and rather than reject certain other thoughts as harmful, you slowly learn to become an observer.

You might picture these random thoughts that come into your mind as having several open hooks around them and being hooked to one another. Each of these has the capacity to catch your observing mind and take it off its object of concentration.

In the process of meditation you are learning how to resist these hooks. That is, how not to become attracted by a particularly pleasing thought which may pull you away from your center. For example, if you are concentrating on your breath, you may think of some especially delicious food. If you become absorbed in the anticipated or imagined pleasure, you may get lost in a train of associations about food and completely forget your meditative focus for some time. The untrained mind may also be described as having hooks in it. These hooks are the tendency to reach out and try to grab hold of certain thoughts or experiences which are seen as pleasurable. Thus when the untrained mind meets such a thoughts, the two become hooked together and the force of that thought moving in a particular direction will carry the mind away with it. This will happen again and again in the meditative process. However, gradually you will learn to remember your focus and to interrupt the distracting chain of thoughts sooner.

When you realize that the initially pleasing thought which you would like to turn your attention towards will actually carry you away and lead to other associations which may well be unpleasant, you will begin to resist the temptations to leave your center. For example, you may come to recognize that the thought of food may lead to desires for food, then to the recollection that you have not yet done your shopping and finally to worries and concerns about how to fit shopping into your schedule. The unsuspecting beginner does not realize that by interrupting the meditational focus, by becoming caught up by initially pleasant distractions, he will eventually bring himself to disturbing experiences.

It will be particularly tempting for you to leave your chosen object of meditation in favor of some other thought that seems at the moment more pleasurable. For example, you may even think that another meditational technique is more attractive. If you are meditating on your breath, you may think that meditating on the word "peace" will be more beneficial and enjoyable for you. However, if you become carried away by this attraction to a new technique, you will weaken the tendency to remain an observer, which is what you are trying to achieve in meditation. Eventually, you may become dissatisfied with even the word "peace." You may then decide to move on to a new object. Slowly this haphazard approach to meditation, in which you become attracted to alternate methods, will develop into a careless attitude, and you will have difficulty keeping any particular focus. This confusion can be avoided in the beginning by resisting the temptation to keep changing the object or technique of meditation that you have started with.

You will find in the course of meditation that there are all sorts of doubts, temptations to engage in other practices, and tendencies to become lost in daydreams and fantasies. All of these experiences are necessary in the slow process of bringing these habits into your awareness so they can be examined and discarded.

This process is described in the following example. If you wish to take a trip to a distant city, you may find that after going a short distance down the road, you become attracted by various sights or objects which present themselves. You may get off the road and follow one attraction after another, eventually becoming so absorbed in these distractions that you forget your original destination. Later, when you remember, you return to the highway and resume your journey, only to be distracted again and again at many points along the way. Some distractions may be brief and others so prolonged that they may take years of experiencing various pleasures and pains before you once again reawaken and resume your journey to the intended destination. This is exactly what happens in the process of meditation. You will become distracted again and again, for various lengths of time, until you become sufficiently disengaged from the tempting thoughts to remember your object. Slowly, as you train your mind the distractions will be less frequent and if you are distracted you will return to your meditation object with greater ease.

The way in which thoughts divert us during meditation is the same way in which various allurements and attractions of the world take us from our purpose and goal in life or from the movement toward experiencing greater joy and harmony. In our outward lives we are again and again pulled from our goals by various pleasures. Sometimes we return to our center after a long period of diversion. Learning how to control distracting thoughts in meditation carries over into the way in which you deal with potential distractions in your outer life.

This tendency to be drawn away from your center by illusory attractions constitutes the greatest obstacle to meditation and to peace of mind. Working with this tendency is the central task of meditation. However, there is a second destructive tendency in reacting to distracting thoughts in meditation. This is the inclination to fight with these random thoughts that come into your mind. For example, if you are meditating on the breath and you begin to think of an event that happened earlier in the day, you may try to be very firm with yourself, deciding that you will not allow your mind to become absorbed in this distraction. As you forcefully bring your mind back to your object of meditation, you will find the distracting thought intruding again and again. It seems as though the more you force your mind to concentrate on your object, the stronger the intruding thought becomes, until, angry and upset, you give up meditation entirely.

When you try to force the associative thoughts from your mind, you are actually giving them a great deal of attention. By giving them increased energy you merely intensify their power to intrude. This is very much like trying to force your mind from an itching sensation. The more you do battle with the awareness of the itch, the stronger it gets and the more impossible it becomes to resist scratching. If you simply become aware as an observer of this intruding thought, without becoming overly eager to banish it from your consciousness, you will find that awareness of the itch will simply fade away. So similarly your thoughts will become neutralized or lose their energy if you watch them come into your awareness and then let them pass on without giving them the added energy of a struggle against them.

One student reported the experience of trying to meditate on the word "peace." As he remembered this thought over and over again, thoughts of an opposite nature began to intrude upon his consciousness. He began to have images of war and injury being inflicted on others. This led him to grow more and more determined in his meditation to block out these intruding thoughts and to focus on the word "peace." However, the more he tried to block out these opposite ideas, the more rigid and tense his musculature and body became, and the more they seemed to assert themselves. After some time all he could think of was hate and injury. His entire meditation became disturbed and he ended up even more distraught than when he sat down to meditate.

If, instead of creating a conflict in his mind, a battle within himself, this student had merely observed the intruding thoughts without judging or evaluating them, if he had only given them passing notice, this entire problem could have been avoided. And these thoughts which were latent within him could have come to the surface of his recognition and diminished in power and intensity.

The proper meditational attitude is to watch the chosen object of meditation and also to observe any other thoughts that come before your mind with a neutral attitude, neither being caught up nor being repulsed by them, neither encouraging them nor trying to push them out of your mind. At the same time, do not try to accomplish any particular goal in your meditation but continually cultivate the attitude of bare attention. Simply watch whatever is occurring at that moment during your meditational experience with a neutral attitude.

If you maintain this neutral position, you are likely to experience a very pleasant sensation in your meditation. You may sense it as a deep peacefulness, a feeling of being at home, a mild joyfulness, or as a feeling of purity. Even beginning meditators typically report such a feeling during their first few experiences. You will find that when such an experience occurs, if you try to hold onto it you will lose your neutrality and the pleasant feeling will immediately be lost. This very positive experience can only be maintained when you are not trying to maintain it, when your mind is kept non-evaluative and without any particular expectation. Gradually, as you sustain this neutral state for longer periods of time, you will become more absorbed in this pleasant and deeply peaceful state, and its intensity will slowly expand limitlessly.

Some beginning students become afraid during meditational experiences as they feel themselves letting go of their habitual concerns and worries and becoming absorbed in the object of meditation. Such students are often afraid of losing their sense of "I" or of being taken over by some experience over which they have no control. Such fears are based upon a misunderstanding of the meditation process. Many students have fantasies about what happens in deeper states of meditation and about what might be called "trance-like" states. Meditation should not be understood as a loss of awareness of one's being. It is a gradual expansion of your being and of your awareness.

Sometimes in the initial stages of meditation you may experience more of a sense of self-transcendence or merging than you feel able to deal with. However, be assured that in normally functioning individuals there is a self-regulating process which determines the extent to which you can become absorbed in the meditational experience. You may come to a certain depth of meditation which is unusually pleasant and then find yourself abruptly pulling back or wanting to stop your meditational experience. Such experiences are typical. When you have gone as far as you are able, for the moment, in transcending your habitual self-concept, you will naturally withdraw from going any further. The mind itself is usually able to adjust and be aware of the extent of its capacity for transcendence. It leads you only so far as is appropriate at that time. Thus meditation differs markedly from the use of drugs or hypnosis in which you must rely on some external and unpredictable source of regulation.

Very gradually as you continue your regular practice of meditation, you will find that you are able to experience more and more deeply peace, harmony and joy. You may find that for periods of several days or weeks you become caught up in doubts and distracting thoughts. However, after this phase passes, you will usually experience greater depth in your meditation.

Some intruding disturbing thoughts may occur repeatedly over many sittings of meditation. Only slowly will they diminish in their intensity and eventually become fully neutralized. Contrary to fantasies that many beginners in meditation have, there is no rapid path to *samadhi*, the state of universal, all-encompassing consciousness. This is a very gradually deepening process. Although you will experience its benefits in even the earliest stages, it will take many years to realize the deeper impact. If you wish to become an outstanding architect, think of the years of training and practice necessary to develop the tools and abilities to achieve this purpose. How much more might it take to work with your own mind in developing its capacities to go inward and to come to rest at its center of incomparably intense beauty and harmony. Be patient. Do not try to force this experience, but continue to practice, and slowly, ever so slowly, it will come.

A student, out of ignorance rather than necessity, expects many unusual experiences through meditation; when he doesn't experience any such visions he thinks that the method of meditation cannot help him. This curiosity to know the unusual is a negative emotion which is not useful in meditation.

When a student comes to a spiritual teacher and starts

doing meditation, he also expects his personality to be instantly transformed. If he does not make sincere efforts he becomes disappointed very quickly. He wants to change the method of meditation, thinking that perhaps another method will be more helpful. But this is a play of the mind, and changing the method would not be helpful at all.

If meditation is done at a fixed hour, in one place, for some time, and if the environment is favorably created so that the mind is not distracted, concentration becomes easy; the mind can attain spontaneous control. Control is very important in the path to expanded awareness. I am not talking about control which students impose upon themselves. Real control is not a strain or suppression, but comes of itself, gradually, when one systematically meditates.

An untrained mind suggests ways of escaping from meditation, saying, "I can do meditation next week." Even during meditation the mind may leave the object on which it is concentrating and take a holiday, engaging in one fantasy after another. The mind is a magician which places many temptations before you and creates conflicts. You should not rely on the mind which is not disciplined. Any hunch or psychic phenomena arising out of an undisciplined mind should be rejected; otherwise one becomes a victim of the superficial level of the imagination. One should watch and verify all of one's experiences. So-called unusual experiences should not be relied upon without verification. Any experience which is of an individual nature should be rejected. Cosmic experiences are purely spiritual and fulfilling; they are other than worldly experiences. Non-spiritual experiences are coated with ambitions, ego and selfish desires.

Obstacles in meditation come from within as well as without. Unless vital calmness or energetic quietness are realized, one should not allow the mind to be tossed by momentary depressions and feelings of joy. The unconscious mind is a vast reservoir of impressions, and a student must go through all that he has studied, heard, seen or done. When he realizes that the unconscious brings forward all the known and unknown experiences to be rejected during meditation, he then transcends his individual boundaries and starts experiencing the transpersonal.

Yoga psychology again and again gives importance to one word, and that is "obstacle." All is an obstacle save for peace, happiness and bliss, which are attained when the mind is free from all conditioning. Then posing for meditation is not necessary. One can meditate in daily life, all the time. Meditation becomes part of life, giving one balance, tranquility and equanimity.

III

Mantra

How Words Affect Us

Meditation has been described as a process whereby we take our mind, which is scattered, dissipated, and pre-occupied with worries and thoughts of future and past, and bring it to a center, to a place of rest. There are many meditational methods. In some you watch the breath. You bring the mind from all distracting thoughts and worries to a place of rest, by centering it on the process of breathing. If you are studying Zen meditation, the method that you might be given would be to just watch your breathing and count the number of breaths that you take. And by centering your mind in this way, it is collected from all of its wandering. If you are studying with a Tibetan teacher, he may ask you to sit and listen quietly to the sounds around you and the space the sounds create so that you can become aware of what the Tibetan Buddhists call "void." Often Buddhist instructors might say, "simply watch the movement of your diaphragm muscle. Watch how it rises as you exhale and how it falls as you inhale. Watch its steady movement, rising and falling, rising and falling." These are very simple and practical techniques that teach you how to observe the thought waves and to establish steady mindfulness instead of being scattered and confused by all the demands that the train of thoughts and external events are making on you.

After learning the preliminaries for becoming skillful at meditation, the student is likely to be given a special sound or word, called a *mantra,* on which to concentrate. Mantra is a set of words or sounds which help the mind attain a state of one-pointedness. A dissipated mind needs to be concentrated. Some of the modern cults believe concentration is not necessary for meditation, but actually concentration is essential. Of course one should not practice any method of concentration which is strenuous.

To try and make the mind blank is an unhealthy preparation for meditation. When a student remembers a sound or a mantra, he is unconsciously concentrating on it by remembering it again and again. That silence which is sought by experienced meditators should not be practiced in the beginning, because the mind has always had an object to depend upon. The object of meditation such as mantra or sound is to accustom the mind to concentrating so that it may eventually be led to that silent state.

Begin remembering a thought over and over again, and eventually you will become identified with it and the experience it represents. Anything that you repeat over and over again will have a lasting influence on you. Surely you have had the experience, for instance, of hearing a song with repetitive lines and then hours later or the next day, those same words seem stuck in your mind. You cannot erase them from your consciousness. A boat makes waves in the water and the waves keep spreading further and further in all directions. Similarly, any thought spreads vibrational qualities with a lasting impact on your mind. This is especially so with a thought that is repetitive like a song or a mantra, wherein the accumulative effect is much greater than a single utterance. If you were to remember the word "peace" many times, that thought would stay with you hours or days later. Eventually, it would influence you and become like a center or home base, a position from which you see the world.

A thought remembered over and over can have a great effect on your personality. Sometimes parents implant thoughts into their children's minds. Perhaps your parents told you "You're lazy, you'll never amount to anything," or "You're very smart." Perhaps they said it once or twice each day over many years. You begin to absorb that. You begin to identify with it and center yourself in that thought. You really believe you are those qualities suggested to you. Even if you do not consciously think, "I'm lazy," the waves of that thought continue to affect your attitudes and behavior. At intervals along the chain of associations parading before your mind, perhaps once every hundred or every thousand thoughts comes the thought (either consciously or more subliminally) "You're lazy. You'll never be able to do it," or, "You're really a smart person. You can do it."

When you center your mind with a particular thought that is remembered over and over again in meditation, you are changing that chain of associations. You are replacing some of those subliminal thoughts coming constantly through your mind with another thought that has been consciously chosen to develop your personality in a beneficial way.

The Universality of Mantra

If you are just beginning in meditation, concentrating on a word you choose for yourself may be an adequate method to get you started. But if you want to seriously take up the practice of meditation, then it is helpful to have a particular sound formula that is given by a teacher. It can lead you much further than any word like "love" or "peace" that you might choose on your own.

These words which are passed on by meditation teachers as centers for concentration in meditation are called mantras. The word "mantra" has two components: the first is "man" meaning "to think." Its root is the same root from which the English word "man" is derived. The second is "tra," "that which liberates us from bondage." Bondage implies being caught up with and attached to objects in the physical world. A mantra liberates us from the miseries, concerns and problems that we experience due to our entanglements in the world.

It seems that most of the great schools of meditation use mantras in one way or another. This seems to be a universal idea. In Judaism, Buddhism, and Christiantiy, mantras or repeated sound formulas are used as a way of centering. In the Catholic church, for example, when a priest is transforming the bread and wine into the blood and the body of Christ for the Eucharist, he quietly says a special mantra to bring this transformation about. In Catholicism certain prayers are repeated over and over again, using a rosary to count the repetitions. This is very similar to the mala beads used in Eastern traditions. The Hail Mary and other prayers are really mantras. In the Catholic tradition they are called prayers, but the use of prayer in this way, repeating it over and over again, is essentially the same as repeating a mantra.

In general, prayer is an outward verbal repetition while meditation involves the inward mental repetition of a phrase or sound. A prayer normally is a petition that certain desires be fulfilled, while a mantra is used to make the mind one-pointed and to attain the center of consciousness within. The method of prayer cannot lead one toward oneness, as can the process of meditation.

In the Eastern Orthodox church a prayer called "the prayer of the heart" is used as a centering technique. Christian monks repeat this prayer continuously as a technique which controls the emotions and modifies them into devotion. The Christian classic, *The Way of a Pilgrim*, describes the use of this prayer as a mantra. It was written anonymously by a Russian peasant who describes hearing a sermon in which the priest says that we should all pray without ceasing. He asks the priest how to do this. But the priest is unable to answer him. So he begins a pilgrimage to find a teacher. After a great deal of searching he finally finds a master who teaches him the prayer "Lord Jesus Christ, have mercy on me." He is first told to repeat it three thousand times a day. After several days the teacher tells him to repeat it six thousand times each day. This goes on and on until he is repeating it all the time. Later the teacher instructs him on coordinating the prayer with his breathing and heart-beat. The book gives a beautiful description of how, after doing this for some time, the prayer begins to take over, repeating itself automatically. No matter what he is doing, the prayer rises up and keeps repeating by itself. As the prayer is remembered again and again, he experiences intense, overwhelming joy. This description of a Christian mystic is a sort of parallel to the use of mantra in the yogic tradition, though mantra is a means which is used for strengthening the meditation. It is important to remember that mantra is not the end but a means.

Gregorian chants, another method of centering the mind which is used by many monks in Western churches, are also similar to mantras. There are mantras in the Hebrew language and in numerous other cultures, including the American Indian.

The Sounds Within

There are two kinds of languages that exist. One type of language is that with which we are all familiar. English, Spanish, Russian, and so on, are all languages we use to communicate with one another. They were created by man and evolved over some time for this purpose. Man created languages through his need to say certain things to others or to accomplish cooperative tasks.

There is also a second kind of language which is not used for communication between people, but for communication between one level of consciousness and a higher level of consciousness. This is an entirely different kind of language, a language more given to us, rather than created. Most people are not aware of this second type of language because their desire for reaching higher consciousness is not intense enough. They are more interested in communicating with others at their own level of development. But when they begin to aspire toward expanded consciousness, they become acquainted with it.

The language which we know as Sanskrit is a close approximation of the purer kind of language which communicates between levels of consciousness. The basic sounds of Sanskrit are related to a higher vibratory state of consciousness and therefore most mantras are in Sanskrit, although there are mantras in other languages as well. Paramahansa Yogananda has said: "He who would track Sanskrit to its lair must indeed end as omniscient." And Panini, a great Indian philosopher and Sanskrit grammarian, remarked: "He who knows my grammar knows God."

In the Holy Bible, at the beginning of the book of John, is the passage: "In the beginning was the word, and the word was with God, and the word was God." Now, that sentence may be very puzzling. Have you ever tried to decipher its meaning? The various mystical traditions agree with this statement and take it literally: the first thing of creation is the Word. Obviously, "word" doesn't mean words as we use them. The words we use every day are a gross approximation of the subtle word. Those who have gone into deep meditative states often report experiencing sounds within. The sounds are not heard with the ears but are experienced just as if they were heard. These sounds are described as exquisitely beautiful and joyfully pleasant. They often resemble sounds we ordinarily hear such as the tinkle of bells, the notes of a flute, the roar of the ocean, and so on. They may be so pleasing that the meditator becomes absorbed in them and is unwilling to withdraw from the experience. The music we create and enjoy is an attempt to approximate these subtle sounds. These subtle sounds are described in the *Book of Revelations* in the Holy Bible. Even beginners in meditation occasionally and momentarily experience these sounds, but not having learned about them, are puzzled by them and do not know their origin.

Even our everyday language reflects a vague awareness of these vibratory states. We often say that when people are truly in love they hear bells. Songs have been written on this theme. The sound of bells is consistently associated with the heart and with love in popular culture, but few of us can explain why.

In the yogic tradition there is a systematic science which associates various experienced sounds with specific energy centers in the body. When one is aware of and concentrates on energy in a particular center along the spine, he becomes aware of the sounds associated with that center. Thus yogis and other advanced meditators have become aware of and have codified a science which describes and explains the subtle sounds within. The sounds which form the Sanskrit alphabet are sounds associated with energy centers along the spinal cord.

OM

There is one sound in particular which occurs in slightly varying forms in almost all spiritual traditions. In the Christian religion, at the end of a prayer, the word "amen" is uttered. Have you ever wondered why that particular sound is used? In Sanskrit the sound AUM or OM is chanted before every prayer. Its sound is very close to "amen." In the Mohammedan tradition they say "ameen," and in the Jewish tradition it is "amen." This is a universal formula which each culture changes slightly to conform to speech patterns. In each case this spoken sound is only an approximation of its more subtle form as it exists in a higher realm of creation. The real OM is not something you say. It is something that is experienced at a higher state of consciousness. Spiritual Masters, in their description of *samadhi*, talk about experiencing the sound of OM and the ecstatic state and knowledge that accompanies this sound.

This is the sound which is referred to in the Bible as "the Word." In the yogic tradition OM is considered to be the vibration from which everything else is created. OM is the vibration which starts out as unity where there is no manifestation. Through the manifestation of the vibration (OM or Amen) in its subtlest form there is a development from oneness into two. It is as if an extension in space, a curved line, is created in the manifestation of the word, forming a division in space on the two sides of itself. Once manifestation of two occurs, there is further bifurcation until we have the physical world which we see before us.

The individual's creation of his experienced world is exactly patterned after the manifestation of the entire universe. His words and thoughts create division, complexity, and disharmony. Meditation reverses the manifesting process by recollecting the scattered investments of energy back toward their source or center where unity is again experienced.

Bringing then the senses all into harmony of
recollection, let him sit in devotion and union.
Bhagavad Gita 2.61.

This manifestation of form from unity is depicted in man-made symbols and in the natural environment through various spiralling forms. The "horn of plenty"—the spiral cone with fruits of creation, depicts this creative process. It is a pictorial representation of creation.

There's a certain curve called a logarithmic spiral that occurs over and over again in nature. It occurs in the forms of galaxies, in the design of the spider's web, in the arrangement of seeds in the sunflower, and in countless forms in the natural environment. You can see this spiral most clearly in the conch shell if you vertically divide it in half and look at its inside. These various spirals have a common form. The same exact curve occurs over and over again. It seems to express a fundamental order in creation.

A similar curve is also created when a wave of the ocean breaks on the surf. Even the sound created by the breaking wave, the roar of the ocean, reflects this curve of manifestation. It is no ordinary sound. Interestingly enough, when you pick up a shell on the beach and put it to your ear, you can hear "the ocean's roar." When you were a child, didn't it seem strange and inexplicable that a shell had the same sound as the ocean? This becomes understandable when we realize that the shell forms the same curve as the ocean's wave. These are, at the physical level, approximations of the OM sound, the seed sound of creation.

This source word contains all sounds or vibrations. It is the mantra from which all other mantras come. It is the word or vibration from which all of manifestation comes. As creation develops, other mantras and the various things of the world come into being from this original source. Manifestation spreads out like a river into smaller and smaller tributaries.

If you were standing on a small creek near your home and had not visited rivers or the ocean, you might not be aware of the way this water merges with other tributaries to form larger and larger unities until they all merge in the ocean. (I remember a three year old child standing by a creek overflowing with spring rains and saying, "Look! There's the ocean.") If you had a stream on a farm, your concern might be with how to use your own small stream to water your cattle, or to form a fishing pond. Your perspective would be limited to your immediate concerns. You might not be aware of the larger context of your existence.

Mantra is a sound vibration which gives you a new perspective from a station further down the chain where a number of individual streams have begun to unite. From this station there is greater consciousness and a larger perspective. The various mantras are vibrational states of consciousness that stand between you and that highest state where you are conscious of unity and bliss. By concentrating your mind upon a mantra, you are placing yourself in a new position further on down the stream. You are collecting yourself just as the water is being collected to form the rivers and ocean.

The Origin of Mantras

You may wonder how we know about these mantras. The mantras are experienced by sages in the highest states of enlightenment when they go to those stations, those perspectives along the way toward unity. When these seers transcend their own finite individuality and go to cosmic consciousness they experience many things: bliss, great knowledge, and many other things we can barely assimilate in our untrained minds. When they return from these states and relate to us at our state of consciousness, they sometimes bring back that "word" or vibration which was experienced. The word is like an encapsuled form or a seed of that experience. Being a seed, that word can actually grow into the whole experience itself. It actually *is* the experience brought back in a crystallized way to the plane where the sage has come to work and teach. This seed is what we call a mantra.*

In order to be a seed of that transcendent state, the mantra must be received directly from the sage who had the experience or from a disciple who has been designated to pass on the word. Some of the mantras received today were experienced four or five thousand years ago and personally passed on through a chain of teachers and disciples which is still intact. In some cases, the name of the first sage who experienced a specific mantra has been recorded and is known even today.

When a mantra is passed on to a student, the transmitter recognizes that he is not personally giving anything to the student. He is simply acting as a transmitter for a spiritual chain or tradition. Like a radio transmitter, he is picking up the sound and distributing it. Since the initiator is only a vehicle, traditionally he is forbidden to receive any personal gain, such as financial return for passing on the mantra.

---

* In most cases mantras are not created by the seer, rather he "sees" the mantra, experiences it, and passes it on to us. Another kind of mantra exists, however, which is formulated by the sage. Usually these are ungrammatical, words with no lexical significance. They are not part of any language. But through his power of being in a higher state of consciousness, the enlightened person can create them. Most of the mantras used for meditation are those that are "seen" rather than created by the sage.

A photograph of a seed which has been placed in a book obviously cannot grow if planted. Similarly, a mantra which is read in a book or given to you by someone who has not been designated to pass it on will not have the effect of the same mantra received through a spiritual tradition. There are books where many of the mantras and explanations of them are given. But to be effective, the mantra must be handed down directly through a sage who has been given care and responsibility for that mantra. Receiving a mantra is an initiation into that spiritual tradition from which knowledge of the mantra arose. The student becomes linked to that tradition through the mantra initiation.

The mantras are not kept secret. They are openly described in books. But the student may be asked not to reveal his mantra to others. This is done, not in order to keep the mantra a secret, but to keep the practice of meditation uncontaminated by the doubts and criticisms of others which would arise, were the mantra brought before your acquaintances. These doubts dilute the effectiveness of the mantra.

There is no difference between the experience of the sage in the transcendental state and the mantra. They are the same. When you repeat a mantra in meditation many times with keen concentration, the mantra takes you to that state of transcendent consciousness. But you may not have such an experience even after years of meditation. The reason you do not have the transcendental experience when you concentrate on the mantra is that you have not yet absorbed it. You have not made "it" completely "you" and "you" completely "it." You are still too absorbed in your small concerns and unable to bring your full attention to the mantra. You just hear the physical sound and you identify with it to a certain extent, but you do not totally realize it. You do not really feel all the subtle vibrations of the word and so you do not have the full experience. When you and that mantra become one, you will also become one with that higher state of consciousness which the mantra represents.

Not all the formulas represent the same higher state of consciousness. Some states of higher consciousness may have more a quality of peacefulness, others a more joyful quality, and so on. The different mantras represent various aspects of different kinds of enlightened states which are preliminary to that ultimate, completely unified state.

The mantra will affect you in many other ways. It helps in dealing with specific problems in life that you have. It changes one's personality by eliminating undesirable traits, and it can protect you from calamity. The mantras given in a valid spiritual tradition will all lead to a higher state of consciousness, but they differ in the manner in which they work at lower levels of consciousness.

Each of us has different needs, circumstances and deficiencies in our personality. For some of us, sleeping too much is a problem; for others, depression. Some of us cannot control our tempers. Still others may be unable to earn enough money to live on or may have a chronic illness.

A mantra is chosen by the teacher, based on the student's personality and circumstances, to help the student with his unique difficulties in life. A particular mantra will make a person very devotional and joyful while being un-concerned about material things, while another may lead to success in the material world. Still another might help someone to resolve internal conflicts and find direction in his life In the yogic tradition, the initiator chooses, from the many mantras which he has been designated to pass on, that one which is most suitable for the initiate's personality and circumstances. The mantra is given much like a doctor would give a prescription.   In this case the diagnosis is at the spiritual level.

Most often the changes are not sudden, but very gradual.   You begin to see problems working themselves out. You find that it is not necessary to wrestle with problems. Things begin to go more smoothly just through being centered in the mantra.   The mantra begins to dissolve disharmonies within and between you and others. You find that conflictual situations seem to go better and that you are not swayed off-center as much as or as often as before.

The mantra is really like a tiny seed that is planted inside of you. If the seed does not fall on rich soil that is properly watered and cultivated through constant use in meditation, the seed will not grow. But if the mantra is used properly with the right attitude, that tiny seed grows into something very beautiful, overrunning the weeds that formerly cluttered your mind, thus transforming your personality.

A mantra, although it is such a small seed, a little word, can have a very, very powerful effect because of the latent power within. Each time the mantra is remembered consciously, it has a powerful effect on the unconscious. The waves of that conscious thought spread through the unconscious as if the mantra were repeated one thousand times. If you consciously remember your mantra a hundred times, imagine the effect it has on your mind and personality.

Those who have worked with a mantra for some time regard it as their home and refuge. It is the place where they can return to from the agitation and turmoil of the world. It is a home base from which they can interact in the midst of confusion all around. The mantra keeps you from becoming lost, from getting so caught up in the narrow perspective of your immediate concerns that you lose your way. Your mantra is your greatest friend. For it is always there to guide you, asking nothing, but giving joy, purpose and direction to your life.

IV

Aids to Meditation

Kriya Yoga

Kriya yoga is described in the first aphorism of the section of Patanjali's yoga Sutras dealing with the practice of yoga.

The word *kriya* means preliminary or purifying. It refers to those techniques which prepare one for more advanced practices. Patanjali, the codifier of the science of raja yoga, says, *"Tapah svadhyayesvara pranidhanani kriya yogah."*

"Austerity, surrendering the self-centered ego to higher consciousness, and self-study constitute kriya yoga." These are the preliminary practices which must be undertaken if we are to attain mastery in meditation. Only then can we have the one-pointed mind free from encumbrances, which will enable us to find that peace and joy within.

In the West, many students think that kriya yoga is a path in itself which leads to expanded consciousness. Actually, kriya yoga is a preparation for meditation, and meditation is finally needed to transcend the preoccupations of our limited minds. There are various kriyas or methods of purification in addition to those given by Patnajali, but these three constitute the first step on the path and provide the foundation for all other practices.

Austerity

Unless we practice austerity we cannot turn inward and plumb the depths of the mind. Without austerity there is a dependence on external comforts and luxuries, and the mind becomes preoccupied with seeking those things. This dependency leads to a weakening of one's will power and the craving for objects. If we don't have the proper cushion to sit on, if we can't take a hot shower, if the daily paper doesn't arrive, if any of our various desires are not satisfied, we become disturbed and lose our equilibrium. Austerity means giving up our dependencies and addictions, freeing ourselves from the demands of the senses and habits we had previously created.

We have created many desires for ourselves and often refer to these as needs which must be met. But yoga psychology makes a distinction between needs and wants, teaching that we have many, many wants, but relatively few needs. Think about the things you pursue each day. How many of these represent genuine needs, and how many are based on desire? Enough food, shelter from the elements, a proper amount of sleep, and similar needs definitely must be met before we can free the mind to go inward. But if we go on pursuing our various desires, we will never find time for achieving our higher purpose, for desires are unending; as soon as one is fulfilled, another appears. Our energy is dissipated in pursuing these various desires. The word used by Patanjali to describe this practice is *tapas*, which can be translated as "that which generates heat or energy." Austerity involves the conservation of energy which is ordinarily dissipated in securing various comforts, and focusing it on the goal of attaining a concentrated mind.

In practicing austerity, it is not necessary to be an extremist. Many people misinterpret the practice and think it involves abusing the senses or deliberately inducing discomfort. Such practices are irrational and are not a part of yoga. In preparing for meditation, we are basically interested in letting go of the insecurity which occurs when we are without external comforts. Austerity properly understood is not self-torture, but the attainment of simplicity and the peace and harmony found therein. Physical austerity involves eating properly, sleeping properly and avoiding extremes of any kind. To regulate food, sex and sleep is a very beneficial practice. Mental austerity is also important. Just as we become accustomed to external objects, the mind becomes attached to building up various fantasies and daydreams. It wanders here and there in conjuring up elaborate plots, romances and tragedies. Useless talking, reading bad literature, indulging in meaningless discussion, thinking about irrelevant matters consciously should be curtailed. The life routine should not be disturbed, but these appetites can be modified. Without regulating these appetites, the conscious and unconscious mind cannot become useful tools on the path of meditation.

Self-Study

Self-study involves looking at ourselves with greater objectivity, analyzing how various things affect us in our day-to-day life, and finally, discovering our true Self. In the practice of self-study, we learn to observe ourselves and see how we are tossed about by our own thoughts and desires, and how we ordinarily react to external situations. We gradually learn to become less identified with thoughts, desires and external forms, and realize our true nature—that supreme consciousness which is behind the various dramas of life.

By observing and studying ourselves, we can correct the false impressions we have built up and come to see things as they are. This process helps us to uncover many revealing truths about the way we function, and opens the way for us to adjust our lives so that we are living in greater harmony with our innermost nature. The process of self-study will lead us to become aware of the more subtle qualities within us such as conscience and will which help to guide and direct our lives properly. Finally, as we go deeper, we become aware of the center of consciousness itself, which is the very heart of our being, animating us and giving life to all aspects of our functioning. At this point, self-study becomes Self-Awareness and Self-Realization.

There are many methods of achieving this end. The systematic recording of a spiritual diary, in which we daily note our experiences in developing our consciousness, the use of retrospection (described in the next chapter) and regular contemplation of particular truths are all aids to the process of self-study. Self-study also involves the study of writings and teachings of those who have mastered themselves and achieved Self-Realization. Such masters are beacons who have truly understood their own nature in its depths. In their teachings and writings they have illumined the way to our own self-understanding. Most of our schooling and reading involves study of a different sort. In ordinary life we learn to develop skills to deal effectively with the world. Self-study leads us to knowledge of the ultimate reality which underlies this ever-changing world of form. Studying the lives and teachings of the great masters helps us to unveil that reality.

When, through self-study, we become aware of disturbance within ourselves, we must also correct those thoughts and actions which cause imbalance and disharmony. Self-study is a gradual process of replacing disturbing thoughts and actions with those which will establish harmony and joy within.

Surrender and Devotion

As long as we are engrossed in our own needs, in "I" and "mine" we will remain insecure. For we are very small, while the world is vast and sometimes threatening. Most of us are concerned with achieving security; we worry again and again, "what will happen to me if . . . ?" Our attention remains focused on what we can receive from the world around us. Our insecurity keeps us from the present moment.

Cultivating surrender and devotion replaces such self-preoccupation with a sense of our connection to that which sustains this entire universe. A sense of devotion and surrender opens us to experiences of being nurtured. We also learn that we have the capacity to become instruments of higher consciousness, serving and giving what we can to help others in their own awakening.

Surrender is often misunderstood. It does not signify surrender to another person, to another limited ego. It means surrendering the limited narrow perspective of self-preoccupation, surrendering a limited consciousness to that larger consciousness toward which we are striving. It means surrendering those ideas and desires which create a false sense that we are basically separate from others and from that all encompassing consciousness that we sometimes call the Divine, God or the Self. In surrender and devotion we reestablish awareness of our intimate relation to that state of transcendent consciousness.

When we acquire anything new we must first let go. If our hands are already filled, we cannot take on anything else. Letting go of what we have been clinging to allows new possibilities to open before us. Meditation more than anything else is a process of letting go, again and again, surrendering all the false and unfulfilling notions we have accumulated over the years which have created a sense of separation from our true nature.

Diet

A young child said, "My little sister picks the cereal she wants to eat by the picture on the box. But I know better. I choose the one that tastes best." As this young child's awareness increased, she was able to go beyond the immediate gratification of visual pleasure and see her choice in a larger context. As her knowledge increases further, she may make still another shift in choosing her cereal, foregoing the pleasure of taste and picking that which is more healthy. If her consciousness expands still further, she eventually may realize that the food she chooses to eat will influence not only her health but her mental state as well.

The food that you eat can be an aid or a hindrance to your progress in meditation. According to the yogic classification, foods are divided into three categories. One category is foods which are stimulating and create unrest, both mentally and physically. They are given the name *rajasic* foods. A second group of foods leads one toward inertia. Those who eat food in this group tend to be tired, lethargic, and lacking in energy. This category of foods is known as *tamasic* food. The third group of foods are those which lead one to a peaceful, calm state of mind, yet provide energy. These are known as *sattvic* foods.

Stimulating Foods
Rajasic

Those foods which stimulate the system to physical and mental activity and toward restlessness fit into this category. Included are such stimulants as coffee and tea, which contain a considerable amount of caffeine. Foods which contain preservatives, including most canned foods and packaged foods, and those which are grown with chemicals also create unrest by introducing toxins into the system.

Those who try to meditate when they have a cold are usually unable to calm their minds. Since the body is filled with toxins the resulting discomfort makes them restless and uneasy. When you ingest various chemicals along with your food, drink alcohol, smoke or take intoxicating drugs, milder but similar discomfort and restlessness results.

Meat is also a food which leads one to be overstimulated, as are spices of various kinds including salt, pepper and "strong" foods like onion, garlic and hot peppers.

Eggs have a stimulating quality to a milder degree and may be given up later in your diet after you have eliminated the more seriously disturbing foods. However, they will provide an alternative source of protein in the initial stages of eliminating meat from the diet. Cheese is also an alternate source of protein although cheese usually contains animal intestine as the substance which solidifies it. (Vegetarian cheese can be purchased at some health food stores). Most cheese also contains a considerable amount of salt.

Foods Which Lead to Lethargy
Tamasic Foods

Those foods which consume a considerable amount of energy in digestion, foods which are stale, rotten or rancid, which have been killed, and foods which have been highly refined all fall into this category. Many of these foods have had the "life force" removed through excessive refinement and have been changed significantly from their natural state. Such foods take a considerable amount of energy from other functions in the body for their digestion and provide relatively little energy in return. Highly refined foods such as sugar and white flour and white bread should be avoided entirely. Similarly, pickled foods and leftovers which have begun to decompose even to a slight degree are poisonous to the system. Preservatives added to canned or boxed foods also destroy the life giving quality.

Foods which consume a large amount of energy in digestion lead to inertia. Meat is a food which causes tiredness and inertia as well as restlessness. Immediately after eating meat, one tends to be quite tired since a considerable amount of energy is diverted toward digestion. Grains, particularly raw grains such as those found in granola but also whole grain bread as well, take much energy for digestion in most people and lead one toward sleepiness for an hour or two following ingestion. The eating of refined sugar may create a brief burst of energy. While meat, highly refined foods and foods which have been kept for some time are to be completely avoided, grains and starches are not as severe in leading to this *tamasic* quality and can be eaten in moderation.

Many of these *tamasic* foods have been introduced relatively recently in man's evolution and his physiological system has not developed to the point of being able to digest them efficiently. The cultivation of grains came late in man's evolution. The refinement of foods is a relatively new innovation. Man's system is not at all adapted to such foods. If you try to meditate or do anything which requires alertness and concentration shortly after eating such foods, you will have little success. You will be more likely to drift off towards sleep than to find your mind concentrated and alert.

Foods Which Give Energy and Calmness of Mind
Sattvic Foods

These are the most desirable foods for human beings. They are easy to digest, give an abundance of energy, help to purify and cleanse the physical systems, and lead to a sense of peace and devotion. The most ideal foods in this category are fruits, nuts and seeds which are eaten in their natural state. Fruits have a cleansing effect on the whole system. It is occasionally helpful to fast on fruits for one to three days in order to allow the system to remove toxins that have accumulated. Nuts which have been roasted and have additives are not included. Raw nuts provide an excellent source of protein without leading to restlessness or to lethargy. Seeds of various kinds including sunflower seeds, pumpkin seeds, sesame seeds, and so on are also excellent foods. Nuts and seeds, however, are difficult to digest and should not be taken in too large a quantity.

Secondary to these foods are vegetables of all sorts which should be taken with as little alteration as possible. Cooked vegetables are not as complete in their vitamins as raw vegetables nor as close to their natural state, however, they are much easier to digest and are therefore recommended. Soy beans are an excellent source of protein and would be included in the vegetable category here. Also, various roots, including potatoes and squash, may be taken in moderation. These contain an abundance of minerals.

Some people think of milk as a non-vegetarian product. Others restrict it from their diet because it forms cholesterol and mucus in the system. However, in the yogic tradition milk is used, as it is a high protein food which contains a wealth of vitamins in its natural form.

A healthful *sattvic* diet would consist primarily of fresh fruits, vegetables, nuts, seeds in moderation, milk products and grains.

These guidelines which reflect the traditional yogic point of view regarding the value of various foods should not be taken as rigid rules about what to eat or what not to eat. You must feel your own way in this by trying certain foods and seeing their effect. Through experimenting with foods you may find that certain foods make you tired while others make you restless. The effects particular foods have on you may not completely conform to the suggestions given above. Each individual's physiology is different. Furthermore, depending on how advanced one is in the practice, one may wish to follow these suggestions to different degrees. *It is not suggested that you try to conform to any of these principles by radically changing your diet.* As with all yogic practices, there should be a gradual evolution from one set of habits toward another. A sudden change in diet will only cause deep physiological and psychological conflicts and eventually a reaction so that instead of progress, regression will be the end result. Begin by gradually eliminating those foods which do the most violence to the system. Then after some time work on eliminating still other foods. It may take years for you to rework your diet.

It is suggested that you begin with the elimination of red meat from the diet, as well as sugar (honey may be substituted), refined flours, including white bread, and stimulants such as tea, coffee, or drugs of various kinds. After some time you may wish to eliminate other meats, fish and fowl, and other foods which are not helpful to meditation.

You should not create conflicts and battles with yourself in trying to eliminate foods. When you have a desire for a particular food you wish to give up, simply substitute another food at that time which is healthful but which you enjoy. A craving for meat will soon pass with fresh fruit or a salad to satisfy your tastebuds and fill your stomach. You will find that it is quite easy to give up harmful foods with this method. Rather than struggling with yourself and saying, "No, no. You can't have that," simply take your mind off the food you do not wish to have by substituting a food that is tasty and helpful. The original desire will eventually fade into the background and give you no trouble.

Prayer

Prayer is one of the most wonderful and useful tools available for developing your personality. Many people do not properly understand the use of prayer. They have been taught as children that prayer involves asking to be given something, that you pray and say, "Lord, make me healthy," or "Help me to beat the enemy," or "Help me to get the things I want." From this perspective it is seen as an appeal to an image of God who will do something for you if you approach Him properly.

As they grow older, many people reject prayer as a means to help them because they have grown beyond this childish conception of prayer. Prayer is left behind like the belief in Santa Claus. This conception of prayer has not been replaced with a more sophisticated understanding of its proper function.

Prayer involves a psychology, a way of working with your own mind. From this perspective it can be seen as a tool to change our attitudes rather than as an appeal to receive something. It is a surprisingly effective technique for reshaping personality.

If you are a mechanic and you want to fix the engine of your car, you must have the right tools before you can even begin to take the engine apart. Tools of one kind or another are necessary in anything you do, without which even the first step cannot be taken. Prayers are the tools for transforming the personality.

If you examine the prayers used by saints or spiritually advanced beings, you will see that these prayers are very different from most of the prayers that people create for themselves. The prayers of these spiritual masters do not emphasize the idea of getting something for *myself* that will make *me* happier. Instead they create an almost opposite attitude in the mind of the person praying. They focus on self-surrender and offering oneself. Instead of asking to be given something, prayer teaches one to be less self-interested.

As an example of this use of prayer, let us examine a prayer given to us by St. Francis:

> *Lord, make me an instrument of Thy peace;*
> *Where there is hatred, let me sow love;*
> *Where there is injury, pardon;*
> *Where there is doubt, faith;*
> *Where there is despair, hope;*
> *Where there is darkness, light; and*
> *Where there is sadness, joy.*
>
> *Divine Master,*
> *Grant that I may not so much seek to be consoled*
>   *as to console;*
> *To be understood as to understand;*
> *To be loved as to love;*
> *For it is in giving that we receive;*
> *It is in pardoning that we are pardoned;*
> *And it is in dying that we are born to eternal life.*

It is obvious that in this prayer what is being asked for is not for oneself. The prayer asks only to be a better instrument of the Lord in serving others. The emphasis is not so much on being given something as on transforming the personality. The general attitude of having something to give and of wanting to give it rather than of being in need and asking is to be cultivated. In addition, a number of specific negative qualities are replaced with those involving giving. The person who says this prayer is affirming his intention to develop particular qualities. Through his own positive thoughts he is trying to transform some of the negative qualities out in the world—hatred, injury, doubt, despair, darkness and sadness. Perhaps you had some arguments yesterday with your friend or with someone at work or someone in your family. If upon awakening in the morning you repeat this prayer, it gives purpose to your thoughts and actions for that day and channels them in a particular direction. You are saying, "I want to replace hatred with love, cease to get into arguments and conflicts with others."

If you say this prayer each morning for a few weeks, you begin to establish this attitude in your mind. One afternoon when you are not consciously thinking about the prayer, you may get into a quarrel with someone. Someone is short with you and you begin to react; you are ready to say something hurtful, and then that thought which you planted earlier in the day comes into your mind: "Make me an instrument of Thy peace." You begin to think, "Wait a minute. This doesn't fit with what I said this morning, with what I resolved. I don't want to be like this." So you interrupt your tendency to become caught up in a conflict and begin instead to calm the other person down and try to create good feelings between you.

Similarly, the use of the prayer begins to create harmony within yourself. Where there is a tendency to feel hatred, to feel doubt or despair, you become aware of these feelings and interrupt them with feelings which cultivate love, faith and hope. The negative qualities within are also being replaced. The conflicts that you experience in the world are the same conflicts that you experience within yourself. The person who tends to be critical of others is merely reflecting a tendency to be critical of himself. When you begin to heal the splits between you and others, you also begin to heal the splits within yourself. When you heal the splits within yourself, it follows that the splits and conflicts you have in the world will also be harmonized.

After a few months of saying this prayer every day, you begin to take on these qualities that you have sown in your subconscious mind through daily repetition. When the opposite tendencies come upon you, it is jarring. You observe yourself and pull back from your old style of reacting. Through the perspective of the prayer, you have created a calm center within yourself from which you can evaluate and deal with your emotional and irrational tendencies. As you work in controlling these negative tendencies, they become more and more faint.

The prayers of the masters universally reflect their humbleness. Through repetition of the prayers this attitude and state of mind is passed on. These prayers develop the attitude that I am not the most important thing in the world, but there is something infinitely greater. For example, the Lord's Prayer begins: "Our Father who art in heaven, Hallowed by *Thy* name. *Thy* kingdom come. *Thy* will be done." The emphasis, as with all prayers given to us by those who are more enlightened, is on the glorification of God rather than self. This prayer does not start out, "Please give me this." It does not emphasize *my* will and *my* kingdom, *my* position and possessions, *my* corporation and family. It suggests being receptive to others and seeing your proper relationship in the world instead of plunging ahead over all obstacles to your ego.

Each phrase of this prayer can have a tremendous effect on your attitude. If you just take one phrase and repeat it to yourself several times each day: "Thy will be done, Thy will be done, Thy will be done," and think about the meaning of it, you can learn a great deal about your way of relating.

If as a habit you begin each day with this resolve, "Thy will be done," then trying to assert your will over others, trying to use others, having the feeling that no one else is going to get in your way and wanting things to be your own way, begin to drop away. As you begin to become sensitive to your tendency to over-assert yourself, much of your behavior is modified. The attitude of this prayer is similar to that reflected in the last line of the St. Francis prayer, "For it is in dying that we are born to eternal life."

Working with this prayer will develop in you a more humble attitude. It will create in you less of a sense of struggle with the world   Rather than being an individual who feels separate and asserts himself against the world, it will lead you to being more trusting and receptive, and then you will experience greater harmony. This prayer, like the prayer of St. Francis, also develops the quality of forgiveness.

The attitude of being in harmony with something larger

and more significant than yourself is also reflected in the psalms of the Old Testament. If these psalms are meditated upon, your experience of the world will be changed. For example, the 23rd psalm begins:

The Lord is my shepherd; I shall not want.
He maketh me to lie down in green pastures;
He leadeth me beside the still waters . . . .

The repetition of this psalm each day can lead you from an attitude of uncertainty, fear, restlessness and conflict to a feeling and experience of being taken care of, of being at peace within and of knowing that you are being helpfully guided.

If, at your particular stage of development, the attitudes suggested in these prayers do not seem helpful, you may choose a prayer of your own to work with. If the idea of God as a shepherd is foreign to you, you can pick a resolve which more properly fits your own needs.

Whatever attitude you wish to cultivate can be developed with this method. If the concept of prayer is still somewhat uncomfortable to you, you can work with this method of using some suggestion that you repeat to yourself each day. However, prayers are more likely to be helpful than suggestions because they incorporate the wisdom of very advanced spiritual teachers about the attitude which is being cultivated. Choose that prayer or idea which best helps you to develop those aspects of your personality needing the greatest change. You will begin to see change through this method in a very short time. Even a week of saying one of these prayers every day can have a significant effect on your personality. The key to success with this method is to use the same prayer regularly every day so that it becomes embedded within, so that the concepts involved come forth when needed through the day. A prayer you choose to use should be repeated at the same time each day so that it becomes a habit. As you work steadily with a prayer, after some time you will truly begin to incorporate those attitudes embodied within it. In this way, it will become a part of your mind throughout your day.

Take one prayer and repeat it every day. The best time is in the morning. Do this for two weeks and observe the effect it has on your personality. Do this as an experiment with the attitude that if you see no results in two weeks you will discontinue the practice, but if it turns out to be helpful, you will continue.

Prayer can be used in conjunction with mantra to work on specific attitudes which you wish to cultivate. While the mantra will also help in developing positive attitudes and in developing your personality, prayer can be a useful adjunct in working on those areas in which you most need to improve.

Silence

We spend a considerable portion of our time talking, but do not truly understand the effect our speech has on others and on ourselves. Seldom do we analyze what our speech is expressing and the effect our words have on our own mental being. If you watch the way you use speech in your own life, you will notice that most of your speech takes you out of the present moment into the past or future. If you meet a friend on the street, you will tend to talk about the things you have done or your plans and expectations. Only a small portion of your words refers to your actual experience of the moment.

While speech can be a wonderful tool for communication to express our experiences to another, it is also a means of covering over experience. We distract ourselves from the immediate situation before us by discussing the past and future. Speech used in this way serves a defensive function in that it helps to take your attention from the immediate experience at hand. It reduces the intensity of the encounter by camouflaging it with dead experiences which have already occurred, and fantasized experiences which have not yet come into being. Words are often used as fences to keep us from being with one another.

We also use words to discuss and evaluate others when they are not present. We gossip about one person, praise another, disdain a third. We slander someone and build someone else up. Words used in this way create a sense of isolation and separation from others and put us in a judgmental position. Words often create a barrier between us and others.

There is a wonderful technique available to teach you to give up the defensive function in speaking so that you will not use talking to remove yourself from the immediate experience. This is the practice of silence.

If you practice silence for one entire day, you will begin to discover the barriers which your speech has created and will learn to transcend them. You will begin to discover that the things you would ordinarily say are often just a lot of words which are not important. When you do not have words to throw between you and another person, you will find yourself confronted with relating to him more directly. Silence may feel awkward if you have become accustomed to contacting others with your speech. But those who have practiced silence report that after the initial awkwardness, they begin to relate to the other person more completely. They share things in a way that they had not before. As they begin to feel comfortable in silence, they begin to experience the non-verbal aspects of being in the presence of another—the bodily sensation, the experience of looking, the facial expressions and all of the subliminal and usually unconscious communication that is shared.

One student reported such an experience with a young child. They spontaneously began to play a game where instead of talking they wrote their communications on a blackboard. As they began to draw pictures for one another to communicate, it opened up a new world of experience for them. They began to joyfully laugh and to relate to each other in a more spontaneous and direct way than they had when they were talking. Students who have practiced a day of silence with their family often report a greater appreciation for one another as a result of the experience.

Maintaining silence for a day is not an easy task if you are used to speaking a great deal. Unthinking speech has become a habit and is also a means of dealing with frustration and discharging energy. The impulse to talk is much stronger than many people realize.

A few who are committed to intensive spiritual practices have taken a vow of silence in which they decide never to speak. This practice of silence conserves energy and develops one's consciousness. As with all other practices, the change in attitude is more important than the actual action itself.

One spiritual aspirant took a vow that he would never speak again. At first he remained quite silent and aloof. But after some time he began to write down things that he wished to express. As time went on, he began writing faster and saying more until, after some time, he was writing so much that he was the most talkative person around. Ceasing to talk is a means for reducing the trivial in your communication. Greater receptivity and awareness is developed as less attention is focused on expressing yourself. This man who substituted writing for verbal speech was obviously getting no benefit from his practice.

Speech is important to many of us as a way of dealing with frustrations and discharging anxiety. The extreme pressure many of us feel to talk is illustrated by a student who was particularly talkative and who clearly used speech as a barrier to immediate relations. This student was also trying to over come sexual difficulties and had decided for a period of time to refrain from sexual relations. It was also suggested to him that he practice silence one day to observe the way in which he used talking. After trying to practice silence he came back and reported that it was much easier for him to give up sex than to give up speaking for one day. It is interesting to see that the drive to talk can sometimes be even stronger than the sexual drive, which we consider as primary.

Many people are reluctant to try this practice of silence. They are so accustomed to the comfort of words that they feel unsure about what to expect and how others would react if they were to not respond verbally. However, those who have tried this practice find that these concerns are not well founded. Others are usually very understanding and the experience often is more delightful than discomforting. People often appreciate the opportunity to share experiences together without words.

There are some guidelines which can help make your practice of silence a more positive experience. It is helpful to practice silence for an entire day rather than for a shorter period so that you can observe the effects in a variety of situations. Do not choose a day when you will be alone most of the time, for you would probably be silent anyway and you would not learn as much about yourself as when you are silent with others. At the same time, do not pick a day when you have obligations that require you to talk, for example, a job. Instead, choose as your day of silence one where you are not working but one in which you would normally interact with friends, go shopping or carry out other routine tasks. Do not be concerned that you will not be able to perform your normal activities or be worried about feeling embarrassed. Remember that there are many people who are deaf and dumb who live their entire lives without verbal communication, and that they get along quite well in their everyday activities. Shopping or whatever you are doing can be done practically and efficiently as when you are talking. And you have the added benefit of being more aware and observant of your experiences. Do not alter your normal routine in the practice of silence.

So that others are not confused and in order to minimize awkwardness, it will be helpful to inform those you meet of why you are not speaking to them. If you fail to do this, they may assume that you are angry or upset about something. One young lady surprised me by saying she had tried practicing silence but that it caused all sorts of conflicts between her and her husband. When her husband was questioned, he said, "She never told me what she was doing. I didn't know what to think, whether she was mad or depressed." Those friends or family with whom you spend most of your day can be informed before your silence begins. Others whom you meet during the day can be informed if you hand them a small card which tells them you are doing an experiment for the day by not talking. You will be surprised to find that most people accept and respond positively to your silence when they know what is happening. Do not, however, put demands on others by expecting them to maintain silence along with you.

You will probably also find it helpful to carry a notebook and a pencil with you. This will allow you to communicate those few things which seem important. You will find that it is too much trouble to write all the things that you would ordinarily say. So this practice will help you to pare down your expression to those things which are really essential. You will begin to differentiate between talking, which is superfluous, and communicating something significant.

If you find one day of this practice to be helpful in expanding your awareness, you may wish to repeat the experience. It may be helpful to choose the same day each week to continue this practice. If you practice silence regularly, you will find yourself developing an increasing awareness of the subtleties of your immediate experience both alone and with others.

V

Meditation in Daily Life

It is important to understand how meditation relates to our experiences as we are involved in various activities during the rest of the day. For most of us have only a short time to devote to meditation each day, but we spend many hours in outward activities. We have many obligations and things to take care of throughout the day. We have our work and our families to look after. We are busy providing for ourselves and there are the needs of others to be met as well. For meditation to be of real value it should have some carry-over, and it should provide purpose, direction and a sense of peace and harmony throughout the day. This is accomplished through meditation in action. Learning to apply the theory and techniques of meditation while we are active, allows us to turn our entire day into a meditational experience. Instead of withdrawing from the world to meditate for only a half-hour or so, our entire sixteen or eighteen waking hours can be transformed into a meditative practice.

You may find that there are times during the day when you are active, yet your mind is centered. You feel a sense of peace and calm despite the activity. You may be talking to someone or writing, and there is a sense of peace and calm. Then there are other times when you become restless, worried, distraught or emotional. You daydream or become distracted thinking about what is going to happen in the future. There is a sense of imbalance. As you watch yourself through the day you may notice these two very distinct states of mind. Some of us fluctuate from one condition to the other. Others spend most of their time in one of these attitudes. It is possible to cultivate that experience of calmness and centeredness if we patiently follow the techniques of meditation in action. We can develop that joy which is found in meditation even in the midst of activity.

Some of us would like to leave the restlessness and confusion of the world behind. We would like to go on a permanent holiday, somewhere in the mountains or in the country where we can enjoy peace and tranquility. We think "If only I were in a more serene environment, then I could work on myself, I could calm myself down and begin to feel good." But we don't realize that our most intimate environment is our own mind and that we take this with us wherever we go, in whatever we do. We have to learn to relate to this internal environment, and once this is achieved we can be comfortable in any surroundings in which we may find ourselves.

Some of us tend toward extremes of outward activity, anxiously running here and there, with little ability to find a center within ourselves. We are like a cork bouncing about on the restless sea of the world with little stability. Others of us withdraw to a quiet atmosphere, fearful of confronting the pushes and pulls of the world outside. But the practice of meditation in action is meant to lead us to an integration of these two extremes. It allows us to develop internal stability and to carry this out into the restlessness of the external environment where it can be further tested, refined, and put to effective use.

Imagine yourself lost in the woods. You wander about in one direction and then another, hoping to make your way out. You follow a path, thinking that it may lead you out, but it twists and turns and eventually, dejected and frustrated, you find yourself back at your starting point. So you go off in a new direction, but you are unable to stay on course, and later realize that you have been walking in circles. You begin to feel hopeless, thinking that perhaps you will never get out. If only you had the simplest of devices: a compass.

A compass is a very intriguing instrument. Have you ever noticed the kind that is sometimes found above the dashboard in a car? As you are driving and turn a corner this type of floating compass seems to turn as well. Before, say, it indicated "East" and now it shows "South." But actually if you think for a moment, you will find that the center, the floating part of the compass with the marking on it, never turns at all. It always faces the same direction. Your car simply turned around it so that now you are seeing it from a different side, the side with the "S" on it.

In our everyday living many of us wander about lost; we try one path and another, often repeating our steps. But a meditative attitude can be a compass for our lives. It can provide us with the reference point, the center from which our actions can derive stability and direction.

A compass sitting on a shelf is of little use. On the other hand, being lost without one can be a nightmare. A compass has its proper function and purpose in the context of the world. When used in the right situation it serves as a guide and even brings comfort and security. Meditation without application to our everyday living is limited. Experiencing the world without a center can lead to all the anxieties one feels when lost in a dark forest. Together, meditation in the context of action can guide us and transform our experiences into a joy. Just as the compass is made for and used in our activities in the world, so meditation is meant to be used as a guide to our actions.

When we apply what we learn about controlling our mind in meditation to our life in the world, we find our experiences becoming transformed. Every action will become part of our meditational experience. There will be little difference between sitting down quietly in a closed room and meditating, and interacting with husband, wife, or friends, or working at our job. We can learn how to be in a meditative state during those times of activity as well as when we withdraw ourselves to sit in meditation.

You might say these seem like two very different things. When you meditate you are quiet, there is little coming in through the senses to disturb you. When you are active in the world your mind isn't withdrawn, you're actively doing things and concentrating on these activities. How is it possible that the two can be the same?

Common Aspects of Meditation and Meditation in Action

There is actually little difference between the way we master our thoughts during meditation and the way we must learn to deal with ourselves in the midst of actions. The ways are basically the same. Consider what happens in meditation. You sit still, withdrawing your awareness from the external world, and attempt to center yourself on a single experience, such as awareness of your breath or a mantra. As you become more and more absorbed in it, you leave your restlessness and preoccupations behind. It is a very simple thing that you are doing, but it is very difficult, because many other thoughts that are embedded in your memory come into your awareness. The hopes, expectations, fears, joys, the unhappy moments, all sorts of things from your unconscious mind come before you as you sit down and meditate. They distract you and disrupt your tranquility. The practice of meditation is a process of learning how to remain centered even though such thoughts come to mind. As we advance in meditation we learn not to be disturbed by these thoughts. Instead of becoming involved with them, we just observe them.

Dealing with the world outside in meditation in action is essentially the same process. Here you learn to center your mind on a particular thought in the midst of your activities. In this case the disrupting thoughts do not come only from your memories and occasional stimuli, but the situation is a much more complex one. All sorts of suggestions, events and melodramas bring new input from the external world into our conscious mind. Many of these also release additional memories of past experiences which are brought into our awareness.

Quantitatively there may seem to be more to deal with when we are actively involved in the world, but qualitatively there is little difference. Thoughts are thoughts whether they occur primarily as a result of past stimuli or as a reaction to present stimuli. And the process of meditation is in each case learning not to identify with or to become absorbed in those thoughts that come to mind, however few or many they may be.

Meditation in action seems more difficult because of the complexity and quantity of stimulation with which we must deal. In a sense, sitting meditation might be thought of as a simplified preliminary practice. The complexity is purposely reduced so that we can find our center and learn how to watch and relate to our thoughts. When we learn to play an instrument we do not begin with complex compositions but work separately with the many components involved—fingering, scales, rhythm and so on. Eventually we must also deal with the world itself in all its complexity just as the accomplished musician must learn to play an intricate piece. The more we evolve in our meditational practice the more we become interested in applying what we are learning to the complexity of our living situations. We have learned to some degree to remain aware of the compass needle, now we take our instrument with us as we move about.

Applying meditation to action is like being aware of two channels at once. You take part in and notice your actions, at the same time you maintain awareness of a center within. That center can be a mantra, watching your breath, or another focus which is used as a stable reference point. Even though there is an outward activity you remember that center and remain calm. You are like a wheel. The outermost part is spinning rapidly but its center is still. As long as you identify with the outer rim you are restless and agitated, but when you identify with the hub you are at peace. The behavior you engage in and the activities that are going on around you are just like the thoughts that come before your mind in meditation. They are part of your awareness but they do not affect you adversely.

In the *Bhagavad Gita* it is stated that even the advanced meditator has many thoughts coming before his conscious mind. But these thoughts do not lead him to become disturbed or unbalanced because he does not identify with them. Thoughts don't disrupt him, don't carry him off from that center so that he throws his weight out onto one section of the rim of the wheel and creates an imbalance in his entire system. Similarly, as we go through the day, if we can have part of our mind focused on a calm center such as a mantra or the breath, we will be able to maintain peace and tranquility in the midst of confusion. If you could observe yourself in your actions from this center, serenity would be yours.

Being in the Now

One of the major principles learned in meditation is to bring our minds again and again to awareness of the present moment. As we meditate, we find our minds frequently wander to thoughts of the past and future. We recall experiences we have just had or those from the distant past. Anticipations, expectations and worries about what will take place also disturb our minds. Each time such thoughts occur during meditations, we watch them come before our awareness and pass by rather than becoming caught up in them. We learn to remain in the experience of the moment rather than be taken over by memories and fantasies. If we are to achieve calmness and serenity in our everyday living, the same attitude must also be cultivated in the midst of actions.

Most of our concerns about the future involve fears and expectations of events which will never take place. Ninety percent of the things we worry about will never occur. We spend a great deal of time in needless concern instead of working in the moment to correct whatever is causing the problem. This absorption in worries and expectations leads us away from the joy and happiness which exist right here and right now.

Paradoxical though it may seem, the best way of effectively dealing with the future is to center on the present and take care of it as best we can. By worrying about the future we merely create added difficulties for ourselves. Our preoccupation interferes with our ability to cope effectively in the present and even creates the future difficulties that we're afraid might occur. In this way our fears about the future become self-fulfilling prophecies. They themselves create the disaster that's ahead of us.

A patient in counseling told me that he had just taken an exam for his high school equivalency diploma. He couldn't answer some of the problems he first came across and began to anticipate failing the exam. He became increasingly anxious about what might happen and started to panic. His concern with how the exam would turn out so distracted him that he was unable to answer the other problems he came to. He later told me those problems were quite easy; that ordinarily he would "breeze through them." But, because of his fears and worries, he was not able to center his mind to deal effectively with the task at hand.

Many of us have similar reactions in other situations. For example, when we speak before a group or interact with others we remain preoccupied with how they will respond to us. "Will they like me? Will they approve of my dress and what I say?" Instead of feeling at ease in the now, you become mildly anxious. Your words become disjointed and off target. You lack presence as your mind runs toward what may happen.

As this young man talked on in our counseling session, he became aware of how his concern and fears of the future were interfering with his effectiveness. He made a conscious decision to become unconcerned about the results of his action. He decided it was useless to worry about his possible failure and create this failure through the worry. He would simply do the best he could at the moment. During the next week, he took his remaining exams and reported that, with this new attitude, he was able to pass the test easily. It was the first time he had ever taken a test without intense feelings of anxiety.

Your future is created out of your thoughts and actions in the now. You are continually constructing a path before you which leads to your future. The path that lies ahead of you can be strewn with thorns if your present actions are callous and hurting. But your path can also be cushioned with flower petals if actions in the present show compassion and sensitivity toward others. Worrying about possible thorns that will face you is not the way to eliminate them. But entering into the present moment in order to construct a more positive future is.

We often look toward the future concerned about structuring experiences that will be enjoyable. We spend much of our time thinking ahead to make things as perfect as possible in the future. But, in this process, we neglect the present and spend our time right now in unhappiness. We don't realize that it is our attitude in facing *whatever situation* which may come our way that leads to contentment and joy.

You may create the most ideal situation for yourself and yet be miserable throughout it. Have you ever taken time away from a cold winter to go south for a vacation at a luxurious hotel by the water? You anticipate leaving all of your cares and concerns behind and bathing in the bliss of the warm sun. But when you arrive and sit in a lounge chair by the pool, you find that you are not able to be content. Your mind is filled with discomforts and dissatisfactions. You continue to think ahead towards what you will be doing the next hour, the next day and the next week. Joy and happiness do not reside in the external situation but in our attitude of mind and our ability to fully experience what is happening in the moment.

Many of us have divided our lives into two categories— chores and pleasures. Tasks are undertaken only because they have to be done. While doing them, we think ahead to the time when we will be finished and can then enjoy our leisure. But these so-called chores can become enjoyable and gratifying in themselves if we can bring our minds to the experience of them. What now seems routine and undesirable can actually become a precious experience. As this lesson is learned our entire life experience will change and the everyday "mundane" things will become a source of great satisfaction. A Zen master once said: "Before I was enlightened, I chopped wood and carried water. Since I've become enlightened, I chop wood and carry water." The outward activities may not change with the expansion of consciousness but the same activity is experienced in an entirely different way. If we could be more completely in the moment, we would find many of the things happening around us, which are taken for granted and seem dull and uninteresting, have a great beauty, harmony and perfection.

Have you ever watched a young child doing the dishes? To an adult, this task is seen as drudgery. But, to the child, the experience of watching the water flow across his hands, dipping a dish in the soap-filled water and wiping it dry later is a great pleasure. For the child is immersed in the experience of the task at hand. His mind is not racing ahead to an anticipation of the future.

What is being done is of little matter but how it is being done is vital. Any activity which is done with the attitude, "I have to do this. I'll just rush through it as fast as I can then I can have some fun after I finish" will be unenjoyable. Furthermore, it creates a mind-set which carries over to all of one's actions. You may think, "I must quickly buy some stamps, go to the drug store and then shop for groceries but, when I get home, I can relax." When it comes time to sit down and relax, you will find that you have created a particular mental posture and relaxation is just not possible. For you carry over the attitude of rushing and being future-oriented that you created earlier in the day.

If you want to experience more peacefulness, relaxation must be practiced in *every* action. You can't rush through the day and then anticipate that you can suddenly change your attitude and frame of mind to become peaceful. Thus, seemingly unimportant actions are just as significant as what we would ordinarily consider "important" ones. If the attitude is developed of respecting the former then the latter will also be carefully done. If, however, the small activities of the day are neglected, when something important comes along it will not be handled with the proper care and respect. For we will not have learned how to act with awareness. Thus, being open and warm with a friend will not easily follow from rushing through our chores quickly. Relating with more awareness and sensitivity, however, becomes almost automatic when tasks as small as folding a letter are performed with care. The person we are in each small activity is the same type of person that we find involved in the larger task. Care in the small things will inevitably lead to care and grace in other activities.

Bringing such care into one's life also leads to increased efficiency. When we rush through activities simply to get them finished, they're often not done properly the first time and then we spend a great deal of energy retracing our steps. Have you ever been carrying a handful of pins when you accidentally drop one? In your impatience and hurry you stoop down to pick it up but, in the process, you spill all of the others you were carrying. How many times in rushing about have you created greater complications for yourself?

It is only by slowing down and paying attention to each moment that such chaos and confusion can be avoided. Once we learn to focus the mind on the task at hand, concentration improves to such an extent that performance of any task is enhanced Through such care and patience, we can accomplish anything. If we wish to do things skillfully, efficiently and with success, it is necessary to develop such an attitude of care in each activity.

Here, having care does not imply being overly involved
or overly emotional about what you are doing; it means a
constant process of bringing mindfulness, greater sensitivity,
awareness and gentleness to each and every experience.
As you work toward developing such care, you will find that
old habits return. Your mind will turn towards anticipation
of the future again and again. But (just as in your practice
of sitting in meditation), refuse to become involved in these
intruding thoughts. Simply watch how the mind loses awareness of the present to become, momentarily, caught up in the
future.   Then allow your mind to once again rest on the
moment at hand. You can slowly train your mind to reside
more and more in the present. Progress is made in tiny steps.
But, as drops of water gradually accumulate one by one in
a large vessel, so eventually your attitude and whole being
can be transformed through this practice.

As you slow down your pace to experience the moment
and become more aware of the activities you are involved in,
you may find that there is not enough time to do all that
you had been doing and still maintain your awareness and
appreciation of the moment. But as your awareness increases
you will also begin to realize that many of your activities
are not really necessary.   They are carried out in a vain
attempt to seek the pleasure and gratification that you do
not have because we are not in the moment. As you bring
your consciousness more completely into the present, you
will find the satisfaction and joy that you have been seeking
by running here and there. Thus, your need to seek out
"pleasurable" activities will decrease.

You will come to find that the activities which are
necessary are quite few and that these few activities can bring

all the joy, harmony and peace that you have wished for. You will come to see that you have few needs but many wants. These wants are created out of seeking an illusory happiness in the future. When you find your happiness in the present moment, such wants will diminish. As you slow down and become aware of your activities and experience that joy and spontaneity inherent within the moment, your desires will decrease. As the desires decrease, there will be more time to pay even greater attention to the moment. You will then find that the most simple things in life are vastly rewarding. The most complete joy is contained in that simplicity rather than in the complexity created by our many desires. This truth is beautifully expressed by an old Shaker hymn:

> 'Tis the gift to be simple, 'tis the
> gift to be free.
> 'Tis the gift to come down to where
> you ought to be.
> And, when we are in the place just right,
> We will be in the valley of love and delight.

Letting Go

The whole process of meditation, whether it is working with thoughts inside or objects outside, is learning how not to get absorbed in those thoughts or objects so that we forget our essential nature. The core of meditation involves letting go each time we find we have become dependent or addicted. The process of letting go has the quality of a flower which is opening, and this creates a very beautiful feeling. It is a feeling of joy, purity, and innocence. It contrasts markedly with the tense discomfort of clinging. This is what the experience of growth is all about. Growth is a joy, a blossoming, an opening, a letting go of whatever we have been grasping so that we can move out of the past and experience what is fresh and new in the present. When you sit down and meditate and find you are holding unto ideas of who you are, or fears or expectations, just say to yourself, "let go." And do exactly the same in the world. With things that you are holding onto and feel "I have to have it, it's part of me," let go of that clinging attitude. It is not necessary to give up the object outwardly. Letting go mentally of your dependency on the object is sufficient to create that feeling of completeness within yourself and within the moment. Simply have the attitude "I don't have to have it in order to be whole. I can let go and still be full and complete."

Of the many objects we encounter in the world there are some that we are attached to and others that we are not. You may, for example, be attached to your car. You feel "I *need* my car in order to get to work, to do shopping, to take care of the many things I must do each day. What could I do without it?" If your car breaks down you may get very upset, worrying, "What will I do now?" But your car is meant to be an instrument for your use, something to make your life easier. If that instrument becomes a burden and creates unhappiness through your attachment to it, of what use is it? We don't need objects to weigh us down, but to free us so that we can experience greater joy and happiness. When the objects that are meant to free us themselves create concern and unhappiness, then we must learn how to let go of our dependency on them.

Gradually as we progress in meditation we learn to stop clinging to those things to which we have been addicted. We learn to give up the attached attitude. You don't have to give up your car or any of the things that you have. Only learn the attitude that "the essence of my being is not that object. I don't need to depend on it. If I really do lose my car it's not so catastrophic."

All too often we are frightened about losing something we depend on. We worry, for example "what if I can't get to work." But usually things work out, we find ways to work them out, and it's not such a big thing. In fact we might even have a better time of it. We might find that the world is much more pleasant without that thing we thought we really needed than it was when we were holding onto it.

Creating Our Environment

The apparent difference between meditation and meditation in action is the difference between inside and outside. Our thoughts seem to come from within, while our actions and experiences in the world have to do with outside. But actually inside and outside are one and the same thing. The outside is nothing but a projection of the inside. The entire world in which you live really comes from inside. It is a creation that you have made. The job you have, the place you live, the person you live with, your situations and relationships were all created by desires you have had in the past. You could have created a very different environment for yourself. The world you are in now, your current situation, came from thoughts inside. You projected these fantasies, these hopes and expectations, and created a whole environment for yourself with which you now are living. For example, if you have hopes, expectations or fantasies of getting a college degree, you write away to a number of schools for catalogs. Then you choose the college you want to attend. Later you rent an apartment, find new friends, and then you find yourself living in the midst of that environment.

The world outside is nothing but a manifestation of what is inside you. You have created a physical, three-dimensional, solid form in which to work with your fantasies, desires, addictions and aversions, so that you become less disturbed by them. You have provided material for yourself, a form in which you can learn to do that. Through this form you can play out your attachments and aversions and find out if they are really good or as bad as you imagined them to be. As you experience each, you eventually find that it wasn't quite what you expected. You learn to become less involved in that particular desire or you clear your mind of that disturbance.

In order to accomplish anything we need some material. An artist, for example, needs paint, brushes, a canvas or other material in order to create. Without these he could not produce a painting. The environment which we have established around us is the material out of which we create ourselves. Through projecting our wishes, fantasies, fears, we can explore them and realize their insubstantiality.

Yet we often get upset because of the situation we are in. We say, "My husband doesn't understand me," or "My boss expects too much from me." We think the situation we are in is very unpleasant or unhappy. We think negatively about our lives, not realizing that the situation we are in was brought about by ourselves for our own learning.

Learning to see the value of any situation we are in is another aspect of meditation in action. Accepting responsibility for our circumstances and seeing the positive value in them as a learning experience can help to free us from involvement. Instead of losing our center in complaint, annoyance, and rejection, we can learn to stand above our situation. We can learn to relate to any circumstance without becoming imbalanced. It has been said that "there are sermons in stones and in running brooks." When we understand that there are hidden teachings in all situations we will begin to find happiness and joy in all sorts of activities that we thought were mundane or repulsive.

If we could fully understand and appreciate that we are always creating our own reality, and if we could live with that idea, our entire way of experiencing our world would be changed. Instead of blaming others for our situation and pushing off responsibility from ourselves, we would begin to see that when we assume responsibility for what comes our way we then transform our world both in terms of our internal state of mind and the external environment as well. As long as you make others responsible by saying, "They're doing it to me, I have to do this, I have to get my degree, my father wants me to work in his business, I have to do it," the thoughts which make up your internal environment are those of a helpless slave. If you think in these terms you are creating a negative attitude for yourself, and the world that you live in is unhappy, unpleasant and negative. But when you begin to realize that you yourself choose your circumstances, the world takes on a different hue.

The World as a Teacher

Instead of thinking of involvement in the world as an interruption to your peacefulness you can see these activities as opportunities to learn how to meditate in all sorts of different contexts. Each situation is an opportunity to learn how to center your mind despite the confusion and turmoil that is going on around. Without being in the world and in the midst of activity, that opportunity would be lost.

There was once a king in India who was also a sage. He practiced meditation in action and was very developed spiritually. He spent his time actively involved in taking care of the country and did a great deal to improve it. One day a disciple asked him, "How is it possible to maintain a meditative state while you are involved with so many things of the world?" The king said, "I'll show you how it is done." He filled a goblet with wine up to the brim and said, "I want you to take this goblet and walk through my palace. There are many wonderous things to experience—jewels, beautiful women, marvelous sculpture and paintings unmatched by anything you have ever seen." (Just imagine yourself walking through that palace. You would probably be eager to see what it is like and would quickly become absorbed in what you encounter). The king said, "I want you to walk throughout the entire palace and then come back to me in several hours' time, with this goblet completely filled. You are not to spill even a drop of wine." The student thought, "I can do that. I'll be very careful." And so he kept his eyes fixed on the goblet and walked very slowly.

He had practiced meditation for some time and was skilled in concentrating his mind. He thought, "I'm not going to pay attention to all these things around me. I'll just concentrate my attention on this goblet and nothing will distract me." Most of us, if we were given this task, would be easily distracted, just as we are in our everyday life. Something would catch our eye and we would spill some of the wine. But this was an advanced student of meditation and he was able to complete the task successfully. He came back and he said, "I've done it. Does that indicate that I know how to practice meditation in action?" The king replied, "No, that's only the first step. Now this time I want you to go back through the palace, take in every sight and enjoy it all, still not spilling any of the wine."

This latter task is much more difficult. You can go through life so that nothing affects you, but it is also possible to enjoy the various aspects of life while maintaining a center within yourself. When you remember this center continuously you will not become attached, dependent, and swayed off-balance by the world. You can experience the joys of the moment without becoming clinging. This is the path of meditation in action.

There is a branch of yoga called *Tantra*. Most people think that tantra yoga involves certain rituals, or has to do with the relationship between man and woman. But Tantra yoga can also be understood as an attitude toward all of life. In this practice instead of withdrawing from the world, going off and meditating, one uses the activities of the world as a means of centering the mind and expanding consciousness. Here we work with those things that ordinarily distract us. Instead of avoiding experiences with the attitude, "here's something that ordinarily gets me involved, upset, or emotional: I'd better stay away from it"—instead of running away from that experience, the student chooses to become involved in it and learns to develop objectivity in the context of that situation. One may even seek out such a situation and practice centering the mind in the midst of it. From this perspective one should be able to maintain a meditative attitude in the midst of the most chaotic or potentially disturbing environment.

Avoiding involvement in the world may lead to the appearance of peace and equanimity, but unnoticed by others our mind may be turbulent and restless. By confronting the world we can sometimes bring this restlessness out into the open and work with it directly. But we must be careful not to lull ourselves into the belief that simply living in the world is a spiritual practice. We must look again and again to see if we are maintaining that stability, that objectivity, that awareness of the center within.

A Daily Exercise

As we understand the process of meditation in action better, we realize that it is a process of self-study. We study how and when we become imbalanced, learning how to right ourselves and how to maintain stability. There are many useful methods which can assist us in this process. These often involve some kind of discipline in which we can evaluate ourselves objectively. Keeping a diary or a daily journal is useful. Another technique to gain objectivity and balance is sometimes called retrospection. This tool has been used in a number of spiritual traditions. Retrospection is like keeping a mental journal. It involves a daily review of each day's events and is best practiced at the end of the day just before falling asleep.

Simply begin to remember the last experience you had that day. Without becoming involved, let the event momentarily pass across your consciousness. Notice the quality of the experience. For example, were you anxious or relaxed, frustrated or at peace. Then in the same way recall the experience you had just before this one. Be a neutral observer, as if you were watching someone else. Don't become caught up in judging, criticizing or approving of yourself but simply make a mental note of the quality of the experience.

In this way systematically go through your entire day, beginning with the last event and ending with the moment when you awoke. This need not be a long involved process if you do not dwell on any happening, but move smoothly from one to another. The entire exercise should be completed in about ten minutes. To gain the full benefits of this technique it should be repeated daily.

It is not necessary to be judgmental for this exercise to be effective. Simply observing yourself objectively will lead you naturally to correct the imbalances and disturbances in your behavior and thoughts. Your objectivity will lead you back to your center. Furthermore, you will find that it will positively affect your behavior and thoughts the next day. The self-observational skill you are cultivating will lead you to notice and interrupt a sense of disturbance while you are experiencing it. You may find yourself pausing as you discover yourself distraught, and beginning again in your interaction or task with a new centeredness.

A similar exercise may also be practiced at the beginning

of each day. In this case you can spend a few minutes after
you have awakened objectively visualizing the experiences
you are likely to have during the day. If you anticipate
going shopping, what quality will that event have? Will
you be preoccupied? Will you enjoy the experience? Simply
let each anticipated happening pass across your consciousness before you arise and continue on your day.

Only a few of the innumerable aspects and techniques of
meditation in action have been described here. If you are to
experience their value they must be used in your daily life.
For any approach or method to work it must be applied
systematically. All too often we read books or go to lectures
about higher states of consciousness to be inspired, informed
or entertained. We accumulate a great deal of knowledge but
put only a small portion of it into practice. We may be so
busy collecting techniques that we have no time for practicing them. If this is the case, then we are not properly
following the path of meditation in action. For one important facet of meditation in action is patient and persistent
practice. If you practice only one exercise thoroughly
you will find more benefit than learning a hundred
techniques and practicing several inconsistently. For each
exercise in itself can be a path to expanded consciousness
if you will only follow it far enough.

The main building of the Institute headquarters, near Honesdale, Pennsylvania.

The Himalayan Institute

FOUNDED IN 1971 by Swami Rama, the Himalayan Institute has been dedicated to helping people grow physically, mentally, and spiritually by combining the best knowledge of both the East and the West.

Our international headquarters is located on a beautiful 400-acre campus in the rolling hills of the Pocono Mountains of northeastern Pennsylvania. The atmosphere here is one to foster growth, increased inner awareness, and calm. Our grounds provide a wonderfully peaceful and healthy setting for our seminars and extended programs. Students from around the world join us here to attend programs in such diverse areas as hatha yoga, meditation, stress reduction, Ayurveda, nutrition, Eastern philosophy, psychology, and other subjects. Whether the programs are for weekend meditation retreats, week-long seminars on spirituality, months-long residential programs, or holistic health services, the attempt here is to provide an environment of gentle inner progress. We invite you to join with us in the ongoing process of personal growth and development.

The Institute is a nonprofit organization. Your membership in the Institute helps to support its programs. Please call or write for information on becoming a member.

Institute Programs, Services, and Facilities

Institute programs share an emphasis on conscious holistic living and personal self-development, including:

Special weekend or extended seminars to teach skills and techniques for increasing your ability to be healthy and enjoy life

Meditation retreats and advanced meditation and philosophical instruction

Vegetarian cooking and nutritional training

Hatha yoga and exercise workshops

Residential programs for self-development

Holistic health services and Ayurvedic Rejuvenation Programs through the Institute's Center for Health and Healing.

A *Quarterly Guide to Programs and Other Offerings* is free within the USA. To request a copy, or for further information, call 800-822-4547 or 570-253-5551, fax 570-253-9078, email bqinfo@HimalayanInstitute.org, write the Himalayan Institute, RR 1 Box 400, Honesdale, PA 18431-9706 USA, or visit our website at www. HimalayanInstitute.org.

The Himalayan Institute Press

THE HIMALAYAN INSTITUTE PRESS has long been regarded as "The Resource for Holistic Living." We publish dozens of titles, as well as audio and video tapes, that offer practical methods for living harmoniously and achieving inner balance. Our approach addresses the whole person—body, mind, and spirit—integrating the latest scientific knowledge with ancient healing and self-development techniques.

As such, we offer a wide array of titles on physical and psychological health and well-being, spiritual growth through meditation and other yogic practices, as well as translations of yogic scriptures.

Our sidelines include the Japa Kit for meditation practice, the Neti™ Pot, the ideal tool for sinus and allergy sufferers, and The Breath Pillow,™ a unique tool for learning health-supportive diaphragmatic breathing.

Subscriptions are available to a bimonthly magazine, *Yoga International*, which offers thought-provoking articles on all aspects of meditation and yoga, including yoga's sister science, Ayurveda.

For a free catalog call 800-822-4547 or 570-253-5551, email hibooks@HimalayanInstitute.org, fax 570-253-6360, write the Himalayan Institute Press, RR 1 Box 405, Honesdale, PA 18431-9709, USA, or visit our website at www.HimalayanInstitute.org.